Magic Numbers for Human Resource Management

Basic Measures to Achieve Better Results

Magic Numbers for Human Resource Management

BASIC MEASURES TO ACHIEVE BETTER RESULTS

Hugh Bucknall
Zheng Wei

MERCER
Human Resource Consulting

John Wiley & Sons (Asia) Pte Ltd

Copyright @ 2006 by John Wiley & Sons (Asia) Pte Ltd
Published in 2006 by John Wiley & Sons (Asia) Pte Ltd
2 Clementi Loop, #02-01, Singapore 129809

This publication is designed to provide accurate and authoritative information in regard to the subject matter covered. It is sold with the understanding that the publisher is not engaged in rendering professional services. If professional advice or other expert assistance is required, the services of a competent professional person should be sought.

Other Wiley Editorial Offices

John Wiley & Sons, 111 River Street, Hoboken, NJ 07030, USA
John Wiley & Sons, The Atrium Southern Gate, Chichester P019 8SQ, England
John Wiley & Sons (Canada) Ltd, 5353 Dundas Street West, Suite 400, Toronto, Ontario M9B 6HB. Canada
John Wiley & Sons Australia Ltd, 42 McDougall Street, Milton, Queensland 4064, Australia
Wiley-VCH, Boschstrasse 12, D-69469 Weinheim, Germany

Library of Congress Cataloging-in-Publication Data

ISBN-13   978-0-470-82161-9
ISBN-10   0-470-82161-2

Typeset in 12/14 points, Times Roman by C&M Digitals (P) Ltd.
Printed in Singapore by Saik Wah Press Ltd
10   9   8   7   6   5   4   3   2   1

Contents

Acknowledgements

A team of people from Mercer Human Resource Consulting around the world contributed in various ways to the discussion, content development and production of this book. They are:

- Adrienne Bonwick
- Daphne Wong
- Elisa Hukins
- Ilya Bonic
- Kylie O'Hare
- Lee Yoke Har
- Patrick Gilbert
- Prue Weitemeyer
- Shubha Kasi

We would also like to acknowledge the contributions made by Professor Kuldeep Singh, from the Indian Institute of Management Indore (India), to the development of this book.

This book also draws on the rich research done by Mercer's in-house experts in the area of workforce strategies.

Glossary

Absenteeism rate is the number of working days lost in a specific period as a proportion of the total number of working days available in that period.

Absenteeism rate for job category is defined as the ratio between the number of staff absent from a specific job to the total number of staff assigned to that job.

Black-Scholes is a stock option model published by Fisher Black and Myron Scholes, two finance professors, in 1973. It has become one of the most popular option-pricing models and is noted for its relative simplicity, its analytical strength and its efficiency of computation.

Call option refers to the right (but not the obligation) to buy a share or stock for a pre-determined price sometime during a given period of time.

Cost-per-hire measures the cost an organization incurs on recruiting a new employee.

Cost per trainee hour measures the average cost per hour an organization incurs on training its employees over a given time period.

Competency-development expense refers to the costs incurred by an organization in developing skills/competencies required by its staff.

Competitor salary is the salary offered by a competitor company to its employees (the basic composition remaining the same) for the same kind of responsibilities performed for a particular period.

Employee-engagement index   is based on periodic surveys conducted to gauge the opinions of employees. The tool allows management to keep abreast of the most compelling issues facing employees.

Employee stock options   are a form of incentive used by companies to reward and retain their key employees. These options usually have a vesting period — that is, a waiting period before they can be traded.

Finance staff refers to employees who deal with policies and standards pertaining to financial and accounting activities within the organization.

Firm salary/competitor salary ratio   is the ratio of the salary the firm is offering to its employees compared to the salary its competitors are offering to their employees for a similar kind of job profile.

Full-time equivalent employees   refers to the total number of employees working 40 hours per week (or the normal working week as defined by a country's laws). This includes part-time and casual workers, whose hours are converted to their full-time equivalents, and the hours of overtime put in by full-time employees.

HR department budget   refers to monetary resources allocated to the HR department for HR staff salaries and costs, for recruitment campaigns and the use of agencies, and for training and development.

HR staff ratio   refers to the number of HR staff as a proportion of the total number of employees within an organization.

Incentive compensation differential   is the percentage of difference in the compensation of gross benefits and services given to high and low performers with the same job profile within an organization.

Internal hire probability measures the likelihood of an existing employee being selected for a position that is available within the organization.

Involuntary turnover   happens when an employee is discharged or has his/her duties terminated by the organization.

Job evaluation   is a method of assessing the work value of positions within an organization. It provides a systematic, defensible approach for grading positions within a job classification system.

Key employees   are employees who show consistent high performance, exceeding expectations, over three or more consecutive performance periods.

Overtime   is defined as any work done in addition to regular working hours. Regular working hours are generally eight hours a day, and 40 hours per week. This figure varies in different occupations, industries and countries.

Number of training hours   is the number of hours spent by an employee on a training course.

Number of employees/Total staff   is defined as the total number of full-time employees in the organization at a particular point in time.

Payroll staff   refers to employees within an organization who are involved in payroll-processing activities.

Process-cycle time   is the time taken to complete a process from initiation to completion.

Profit per employee   is a measure applied to determine an organization's productivity at the level of the individual employee.

Points-factor evaluation   is a system or methodology used by consulting companies to measure the value of a particular job/role across the entire organization. This system works on assigning points/numerical value to different dimensions of work that are regarded as key determinants of work value.

Relative performance assessment   is a concept in which managers' assessments of the performance of their staff is compared and ratings are awarded relatively.

Response time per request for information   refers to the time it takes to provide employee-specific information (for example, payroll data or superannuation/medical benefit details) when requested.

Sick-leave rate   is the number of employees in an organization who take sick leave within a specified period as a proportion of the total workforce within that organization.

Time taken to fill a vacancy   measures the average number of days it takes for an organization to hire a candidate for a job, from the day the job becomes available.

Voluntary turnover   refers to a situation where an employee leaves an organization on his or her own accord.

Introduction

The human resources (HR) function within any company structure has undergone dramatic transformations in the last two decades. Far from being a sweatshop tinkering mainly with personnel and payroll, the HR function as we know it today has assumed a much more dynamic and elegant form, providing strategic direction for organizational change and business growth.

As organizations jostle in a competitive marketplace to produce more for less, HR will be faced with the onerous task of delivering more cost-effective people programs.

Organizations typically rely on HR measures to build a picture of the following:

- how well HR is operating

- how efficient and effective the HR function is

- how to gauge organizational climate and performance

- how to improve on the productivity of all staff

- how to maximize the return on human capital.

Within any high-performance organization, HR will be required to demonstrate clear links between investments on HR and the subsequent impact on business results. What quantitative measures can HR rely on to build the nexus between HR programs and business transformation?

Having found the appropriate measures, how can organizations then apply the wealth of good data available today to generate reliable information that tells a complete story about which workforce factors are the drivers of a particular organization?

Mercer's own extensive client experience on the assessment of effective workforce performance relies on several fundamental principles. These are:

- **Recognize that workforce management is a form of asset management**, focusing on the procurement, management, and divestiture of human assets based on business needs and performance drivers.

- **Segment the employee population,** beginning with the parts of the organization with the greatest potential impact.

- **Consider three critical dimensions in defining the workforce**:

  - capabilities (for example, demographics, experience, education)

  - behaviors (for example, performance, retention)

  - attitudes (for example, risk-taking, innovation, teamwork).

- **Determine which workforce characteristics contribute most** to the creation of value, at what cost, with what risks and over what time period.

- **Establish priorities and manage the change process** to ensure success in design and implementation of needed program changes (for example, recruitment, performance management, retention).[1]

Over the last decade or more, Mercer has developed a market-leading framework and suite of measurement tools to help companies execute this approach to workforce management.

This book is a basic introduction to the world of HR measurement and will help equip the hands-on HR manager with a comprehensive toolkit of commonly used measures that can be used for benchmarking purposes. But far more critical than simply delivering these benchmarks is the need to integrate them into the organization's overall change agenda. Most HR benchmarking efforts provide descriptive information for the organization; no more than that. A far more meaningful and powerful approach is to use these numbers to build a network of information that can be linked back to the organization's entire information pool to make changes and build predictive or forecasting models to plan for the future needs of the business.

How this Book can Help HR

Magic Numbers for Human Resource Management will help senior managers and key executives understand and appreciate traditional HR measures and how they are currently used. The book will also provide insights into non-traditional measures and how they can all be put to strategic use. The book will help answer the following questions:

- What HR measures are most commonly used?

- Which measures are the most popular?

- Which are the cutting-edge measures?

- What do these measures really mean?

- How do you use these measures strategically?

How this Book is Organized

We have chosen to cluster the HR measures into three core components within an organization's people-management map: Productivity and Efficiency; Staffing and Learning; and Talent and Reward. Each of these components forms an important link in the entire spectrum. Taken in isolation, these numbers have limited application. But applying the measures in a manner that builds context into the equation can provide a potent message for your organization's workforce.

Every measure is carefully defined and the calculations are explained in detail, enabling the reader to put them into practice. We explain why and how these measures have been useful, and how they have been used by companies to gauge both the effective performance of their systems and programs and the efficiency of their HR efforts in this regard.

We have added two additional sections — Appendix 1 and Appendix 2 — to provide readers with some practical information and some recent thinking on workforce management issues. Appendix 1 illustrates how HR can properly monitor specific HR programs using HR "dashboards". This "dashboard", as we choose to call it, seeks to track key indicators to highlight either the success or failure of certain HR programs. In Appendix 2, we present some findings done in Asia on how employees view their work, and a whole host of other factors at work. The findings, as we show, can present highly critical information on how to improve HR management.

Is benchmarking an art or a science? The truth lies somewhere in between. There is some "magic" involved in applying and getting the best out of these measures. Do you meet the norm? Do you set your benchmarks a little higher than average or far above the crowd? There is a tendency for organizations to try slavishly to meet the "norm", as if the norm itself was some magic mantra. True business success can be found in using these benchmarks to meet the organization's over-arching goal — of delivering business transformation. True magic also lies within: looking internally within your organization to use that advantage you have, rather than being led by external market measures to play catch-up. Our concluding chapter helps you draw some salient lessons from the practice of HR performance measurement to truly make magic with HR numbers.

[1] Mercer Human Resource Consulting Performance, Measurement and Reward Business Intranet, 2005.

Part One

Magic Numbers for Productivity and Efficiency

MAGIC NUMBERS FOR PRODUCTIVITY AND EFFICIENCY

Productivity and efficiency measures are among the most watched of the HR metrics and comprise the following:

1. Absenteeism rate by job category and job performance
2. Accident costs
3. Average time for dispute resolution
4. Cost-per-hire
5. Finance staff as a percentage of total staff
6. Overtime hours
7. The HR budget as a percentage of sales
8. HR staff as a percentage of total staff
9. IT staff as a percentage of total staff
10. Marketing staff as a percentage of total staff
11. Payroll staff as a percentage of total staff
12. Percentage of employees making suggestions
13. Process-cycle time
14. Profit per employee
15. Response time per request for information
16. Sick-leave rate
17. Sick days per full-time equivalent employee per year
18. The cost of medical disbursement by category of ailment
19. Time taken to fill a job vacancy

Absenteeism Rate by Job Category and Job Performance

THE DEFINITION

Absenteeism is defined as an employee's failure to report for work when scheduled to do so. It does not include absence from work by prior arrangement, approved annual leave and other statutory vacation days. Prolonged or repeated absenteeism is often an indicator of the dissatisfaction level of an employee as there is an inverse correlation between "satisfaction" and "absenteeism". Absenteeism may also occur as a result of unforeseen circumstances such as sickness, bad weather, or other workplace dynamics such as friction with co-workers or lack of motivation to go to work.

THE FORMULA

Absenteeism is measured as the number of employees who are missing from work as a proportion of the total number of employees.

$$\text{Absenteeism rate} = \frac{\text{No. of working days lost in a specific period}}{\text{Total no. of staff working days available in the period}}$$

Absenteeism rate for job category is defined as the number of staff absent from a specific job as a proportion of the total number of staff assigned to that job.

$$\text{Absenteeism rate (job category)} = \frac{\text{No. of working days lost for specific job for specific period}}{\text{Total no. of staff working days available for that period}}$$

The absenteeism rate for job performance would be the number of staff absent as a proportion of the total number of staff *with the same level of job performance.*

$$\text{Absenteeism (job performance)} = \frac{\text{No. of working days lost in a specific period}}{\text{Total no. of staff working days available for those with same level of job}}$$

The Components

The *number of working days lost* for the period is the sum of the number of staff failing to turn up each day over the whole period.

Total working days available is the total number of staff multiplied by the number of days in the period.

The *absenteeism rate* can also be calculated for a single day to reveal if there is a trend of absences on a particular day of the week. There might be, for example, a "Blue Monday" syndrome, where employees are reluctant to turn up on Monday after enjoying a couple of days off or after a long weekend. This results in an exceptionally high absenteeism rate on Mondays in some enterprises.

The absenteeism rate can be calculated for a specific period — a week, fortnight, month or quarter — to enable a comparative study of absenteeism rates over different periods.

The absenteeism rate in the job category might reflect the degree of strain, inconvenience and distress caused by the job. This rate could be compared with absenteeism rates for different jobs to help determine the complexity associated with a particular job. For example, night jobs have comparatively higher rates of absenteeism than day jobs.

Workplace studies have shown that there is an inverse relationship between job satisfaction and absenteeism rates. The absenteeism rate in job performance might well be an indication of the satisfaction levels, sense of accomplishment and comfort being derived from different jobs within an organization. So absenteeism rates can be used to validate the correlation between higher performance and higher job satisfaction which, in turn, reduces absenteeism.

It is difficult for an organization to carry out its functions in a smooth and efficient manner if its employees fail to report to work. So it's important for any organization to estimate the costs it is incurring as a result of absenteeism. The costs of absenteeism are many and varied and can come in the form of:

- lost production

- a drop in overall product quality where co-workers are asked to make up the shortfall

- having to employ outside labor

- absentees who may be dissatisfied with their work, eventually leaving the company

- lost wages (in the case of sick leave)

- the payment of overtime premiums to make up for lost work

- extra supervision of the problem and of the performance of temporary workers called in to cover

- lost opportunities arising from facilities not being put to full use.

WHERE'S THE DATA?

The data used to calculate absenteeism rates can be taken from the organization's payroll system, which should record both the number of staff and the number of absences in any given period.

CALCULATING IT — AN EXAMPLE

As we have seen, the absenteeism rate is the number of working days lost in a specific period divided by the total number of working days available in the same period.

Example:

a = average number of employees in workforce = 10
b = number of available working days during period = 20
c = total number of working days available $(a \times b)$ = 200
d = total number of days lost due to absences in the period = 90

e = absenteeism rate: $\left(\dfrac{d}{c}\right) \times 100 = 45\%$

To calculate the absenteeism rate for one day, divide the number of absentees for that day by the total number of employees (which can be derived from the above formula when the period is 1).

Example

a = average number of employees in workforce = 20
b = number of available working days in period = 1
c = total number of working days available $(a \times b)$ = 20
d = total number of days lost due to absences in the period = 3

e = absenteeism rate: $\left(\dfrac{d}{c}\right) \times 100\% = 15\%$

WHAT IT MEANS

Having full information on rates of absenteeism could help the organization determine one or more of the following:

- if there is some problem within a particular department where the absenteeism rate is significantly higher than in other job categories

- days where employees are typically reluctant to come to work

- whether there are morale problems within the company as a whole (where, say, absenteeism is higher than the industry average)

- the extent to which performance and productivity suffer as a result of high absenteeism

- whether employees are happy with their current workload and how to compensate those with heavier workloads.

2 Accident Costs

THE DEFINITION

For our purposes, an accident is a sudden, unexpected event which occurs in the workplace, on the way to and from the normal place of work or in a work-related context which results in injury, lost time and/or property damage. Any economic damages/losses that arise from this are typically classified as accident costs.

Accident costs can be of two types:

Direct Costs

- Medical injury and illness costs
- Compensation costs
- Building damage
- Tool and equipment damage
- Product and material damage
- Legal expenses
- Expenditure on emergency supplies
- Interim equipment rental.

Indirect Costs

- Investigation time
- Wages paid for lost time

- Cost of hiring and/or training replacements

- Overtime payments

- Production delays and interruptions

- Extra supervisory time

- Clerical time

- Decreased output of injured worker upon return to work

- Loss of business and goodwill

- Fines, increased insurance premiums or other charges levied against the organization as a result of the accident.

THE COMPONENTS

Direct costs are readily measurable because they represent the amount spent on rebuilding or refurbishing the damage on the property and workers' compensation claims, including lost wages and medical expenses.

Indirect costs include those costs associated with accidents that are not covered or paid by workers' compensation.

Estimating indirect costs

Indirect costs may be estimated using the following guidelines.

Cost incurred by employees who assist injured employees

Certain employees may provide assistance to an injured employee following an accident, including assistance to obtain medical treatment. Such assistance may also include that provided by the workers' compensation claims coordinator. These costs may be estimated by determining the amount of time spent by each employee on rendering such assistance, and multiplying this by the employee's individual rate of pay. In the case of severe accidents, counseling and other support for those who provided assistance may also need to be factored in.

Lost production

Production slowdowns and lost production may occur as a result of the accident such as when equipment is being investigated, repaired, replaced or is sitting idle following an accident. These costs may be estimated by identifying the number of employees who are unable to work as a result of the equipment being out of action, determining the length of time production is affected, then multiplying the employees' time by their respective rates of pay. In addition, in a manufacturing company, the shortfall in normal output levels can be calculated to estimate the related costs.

Non-compensated time of the injured employee

Following an injury, an employee may lose time from work but not receive workers' compensation indemnity benefits immediately. This non-compensated time includes time lost on the day of the injury and, where temporary income benefits are not received, the period the employee has to wait before becoming eligible for workers' compensation. After an employee returns to work, non-compensated time may include time required for visits to the doctor, physical therapy sessions, and other medical care. Also, if an employee elects to receive sick-leave pay in lieu of workers' compensation temporary income benefits, these sick-leave payments should be included in the non-compensated indirect cost estimates. The total amount of non-compensated time should be calculated, and then multiplied by the employee's rate of pay.

Overtime or compensatory time

Often following injuries, other employees may work additional time to complete work not performed by the injured employee. This often results in overtime or compensatory time being paid. The amount of overtime or compensatory time should be included in the indirect cost estimates.

Reduced output of replacement employees

Temporary employees or replacement employees may require a certain amount of time to learn the injured employee's job, and to become proficient in handling their duties. Therefore, this reduction in output should be estimated as an indirect cost. For example, a new, temporary employee may be only 50% proficient in performing the required duties. Therefore, 50% of the temporary employee's wages would be considered reduced output and, by extension, an indirect cost of the accident.

Supervisor's activities

The injured employee's supervisor is often required to perform certain activities related to the accident which prevent the supervisor from performing other, regular supervisory duties. Such activities may include completing accident report forms; helping the injured employee to obtain medical treatment; follow-up visits to the employee while absent from work; analyzing the cause of the accident; and supervising corrective actions. The amount of time the supervisor spends on these activities may be estimated, and then multiplied by the supervisor's rate of pay to determine the indirect costs.

Accident reporting, review and analysis, claims processing, and record keeping

In addition to the usual workers' compensation claim forms, an accident report form should be completed for every accident and incident. This should include a thorough review and analysis of the causes of the accident. All forms relating to an accident should be maintained in an information system that includes a complete and accurate record of each accident, incident and workers' compensation claim. All costs associated with developing, reviewing and maintaining these records should be included in the indirect cost estimates.

First-aid costs

The costs associated with first-aid supplies that may be used to treat an injured employee are considered indirect costs and should be included in the indirect cost estimates.

Return-to-work program costs

The administrative costs of a return-to-work program are considered an indirect cost of accidents. Therefore, all such costs, including employees' salaries, supplies, equipment and office space should be incorporated into the indirect cost estimates.

Although relevant data on indirect accident costs is difficult to collect, the best estimate for each of the components outlined above should be determined for a specified period of time. For example, the data may be collected for a six-month period of typical workers' compensation claims experience. After the data have been collected for this period, a ratio of indirect to direct costs can be calculated. This process should be repeated as appropriate to update the typical ratio of direct to indirect costs.

Amount paid in insurance premiums

This is the amount the firm pays annually to insure its plant, materials and personnel against accidents and subsequent losses.

In quantifying accident costs, it helps to classify accidents into the following categories:

- accidents when employee takes time off work

- accidents when employee is not off work

- accidents resulting only in damage to property.

Average cost associated with each type of accident

The different categories of accidents mentioned above carry different types and magnitudes of direct and indirect costs. Therefore, computing the average cost for each type of accident seems to be more realistic and would give a closer estimate of the total accident cost.

THE FORMULA

It is difficult to present a standard formula for estimating accident costs, but one approach is described below.

To estimate costs associated with a particular incident, we may separate the costs into the different categories mentioned above and calculate the impact of each category separately. The total costs associated with that accident would then be represented by the sum of all the categories.

Direct costs associated with an accident are readily measurable but indirect-cost data are considerably more difficult to obtain because the information is not often captured or quantified as it accrues. Although difficult to measure, it is still important to estimate indirect costs because they are usually several times greater than direct costs.

Indirect costs are usually expressed as a ratio to direct workers' compensation costs, such as 4:1. That is, for each dollar of direct cost, there is a corresponding indirect cost of four dollars. While there is no preset formula or method for estimating indirect costs, an organization may find it useful to develop its own indirect accident cost ratio that more accurately reflects its own experience and is appropriate to its own operations. This ratio may then be used as an estimator of the total cost.

Where's the Data?

The data used for deriving these estimates lie mostly in the company's financial statements and in the accident and workers' compensation records required by law and/or the organization's internal policies. Financial statements, such as the cash-flow statement, should give the figure for the company's insurance premiums. Accident records should provide data regarding the type and number of accidents and the direct claims or damages arising from each. Employee compensation records should provide the information required to estimate the average accident cost per employee. Finally, the payroll system will give the total number of employees in the workforce.

CALCULATING IT — AN EXAMPLE

Estimating total cost associated with an accident:

Indirect costs ratio (worked out on the basis
of the company's past experience) = 4:1

Direct costs	= US$2,000
Indirect costs	= US$2,000 × 4
	= US$8,000
Total accident cost	= US$2,000 + US$8,000
	= US$10,000

The estimates provided using these tools are based on average values. They only provide an indication of how much accidents could cost an organization each year. Accident costs are also correlated with:

- the adequacy of health-and-safety controls

- the adequacy of risk management for employees

- technology employed by the organization

- the staff costs

- the value of the products or services generated.

WHAT IT MEANS

Accident costs can be analyzed against a number of benchmarks (such as historical trends within the organization, business units, industry or geographic averages, and so on). Regardless of the benchmark used, accident costs which appear to be increasing and/or outside acceptable limits may indicate some of the following:

- preventative measures inside the company are inadequate

- staff recruitment, training, supervision and/or morale require attention

- technology, equipment, work processes, and/or work environment require attention.

Even if an organization's accident costs appear to be in line with relevant targets, there will always be opportunities to reduce the incidence and severity of accidents and the costs associated with them. The benefits of such reductions will have a direct impact on the organization's financial results and, more importantly, on how the organization manages its workforce.

3 Average Time for Dispute Resolution

THE DEFINITION

The time for dispute resolution is the length of time for which a dispute continues to exist in an organization. The shorter the resolution time, the more effective the dispute-resolution process.

THE FORMULA

$$\text{Average time for dispute resolution} = \frac{\text{No. of days taken to resolve disputes}}{\text{Total number of disputes}}$$

THE COMPONENTS

Organizational disputes are defined as conflicts, both internal as well as external, that are taken to a court of law. The total number of disputes is the number of disputes arising in an organization in a given financial year. For our purposes, let's use one year as the average time taken to resolve a dispute.

WHERE'S THE DATA?

Dispute-resolution data can be found in the company's records of industrial or legal proceedings. There are two main measures: the number of disputes and the "days taken". The latter can be calculated simply from the commencement of the dispute until the dispute is settled.

CALCULATING IT — AN EXAMPLE

Record of disputes at ABC Inc. in 2004

Dispute number	Started (dd/mm/yyyy)	Settled (dd/mm/yyyy)	Total days
1.	01/02/2004	02/03/2004	31
2.	22/02/2004	30/03/2004	38
3.	22/04/2004	12/08/2004	113
4.	19/07/2004	07/01/2005	173
5.	11/10/2004	12/01/2005	94

Sum of number of days taken
to resolve disputes
$$= 31 + 38 + 113 + 173 + 94$$
$$= 449$$

Total number of disputes $= 5$

Average time of dispute resolution $= \dfrac{449}{5}$

$$= 89.8 \text{ days}$$

WHAT IT MEANS

The trend provides an organization with information regarding the effectiveness of its dispute-resolution system. The longer it takes to settle a dispute, the more costly it is. It is important, therefore, for the organization to take measures to reduce the dispute-resolution time.

Where the data indicate that the average resolution time is increasing, this should signal to the company that it has a problem in this area.

Cost-per-hire

THE DEFINITION

Cost-per-hire (CPH) is a metric that indicates the costs an organization incurs on recruiting a new employee. It is calculated by dividing the total staffing costs by the number of hires and is an important component of an organization's staffing costs.

THE FORMULA

$$CPH = \frac{(AD + AF + ER + T + Relo + RC + 10\%)}{NH}$$

where

AD represents advertising costs
AF are agency fees
ER are employee referral costs
T is travel expenses
Relo is relocation costs for the new hire
RC represents the fully loaded cost of all recruiter's time
10% is an illustration of the common calculation for all
overhead and administrative support, which will vary
for different companies and locations.
NH is the number of new hires

THE COMPONENTS

The components of CPH can be categorized as internal costs, external costs, candidates' interview expenses, and direct fees.

Internal costs refer to the costs incurred by the company's personnel in conducting such activities as reviewing résumés and interviewing candidates or in traveling on recruiting trips. They would also incorporate overtime paid to other employees who are working extra to cover for an existing vacancy.

External costs are the fees paid to an outside recruiting agency, while any money spent on candidates' travel expenses or on setting up video interviews, as well as on lodging, meals and relocation expenses of the successful candidate, would all be included under the *candidate interview* category.

Finally, *direct fees* cover the costs associated with advertising, job or campus recruitments/fairs, and bonuses offered to employees for new referrals.

WHERE'S THE DATA?

The costs can be found in the company's accounts and the organization's employee database will keep track of all new hires.

CALCULATING IT — AN EXAMPLE

Number of new recruits	= 10
Advertising agency costs incurred	= $2,000
Agency fees	= $3,000
Employee referral costs	= $3,000
Travel expenses	= $1,000
Relocation expenses	= $1,500
Internal recruiter's costs	= $1,000
Administrative costs (10%)	= $1,150

$$\text{CPH} = \frac{(2{,}000 + 3{,}000 + 3{,}000 + 1{,}000 + 1{,}500 + 1{,}000 + 1{,}150)}{10}$$
$$= \$1{,}265$$

WHAT IT MEANS

A declining cost-per-hire figure may indicate that web-enabling technology has provided the company with a more cost-efficient means for recruiting employees. Thus, the company may be spending less on traditional means of advertising, such as through newspapers.

An increasing cost-per-hire figure might indicate that the company's suppliers' costs (from recruitment agencies, for example) may be rising, raising the need to review the cost-effectiveness of commercial contracts. Where the number of new hires recruited through traditional methods is declining, this perhaps points to the need to reassess the recruitment strategy.

Finance Staff as a Percentage of Total Staff

THE DEFINITION

This measures the number of employees who deal with the organization's finances, from the accounting clerk to the chief financial officer. It indicates the resources the organization is investing in taking care of and analyzing its financial data.

THE FORMULA

Finance staff as a percentage of total staff

$$= \frac{\text{No. of finance staff}}{\text{Total no. of staff}} \times 100\%$$

THE COMPONENTS

The *finance staff* develop and promulgate policies and standards pertaining to financial and accounting activities within the organization and review their implementation.

Total staff is the total number of full-time equivalent employees employed by the organization at a particular time.

WHERE'S THE DATA?

This information is recorded in the company's payroll system.

CALCULATING IT — AN EXAMPLE

Finance staff   = 200

Total staff   = 2,700

Finance staff as a
percentage of total staff $= \dfrac{200}{2,700} \times 100\%$

$= 7.4\%$

WHAT IT MEANS

If the ratio is increasing, this may suggest that the organization's financial operations are becoming more complex, and this may require more in-depth analysis. With the growing importance and need for more precise and regular financial information for decision-making purposes, the ratio will tend to increase. The ratio tends to increase as the processing of transactions becomes more detailed and complex or when control and reporting requirements are increased. But an increase may also indicate a need to review work practices, the possibility of overstaffing or the need to investigate better technology or outsourcing options.

A decrease in the ratio, on the other hand, is typically regarded as a positive organizational outcome that may simply be a result of better leverage of the finance function across a larger population of workers. Alternatively, it may be the result of improvements in work practices and technology that require fewer staff.

MAGIC NUMBER

6

Overtime Hours

THE DEFINITION

Overtime is defined as any work done in addition to regular working hours. Depending on the statutory requirement, regular working hours are generally eight hours a day, and 40 hours per week. This figure varies in different occupations, industries and countries. This information can be used, on the one hand, to calculate labor efficiency and, on the other, to calculate any additional penalty payments beyond contracted rates.

Extended working hours affect both the employee and the company. Therefore, solutions that seek to better manage how, when and under what circumstances long hours of work are necessary must include both workforce and management. Having this information helps the management to plan its resources to achieve an optimal balance between maximizing the use of resources, responding to workload demands and preventing fatigue. Overtime may vary at different times of the year in response to significant changes in demand patterns at different seasons.

THE FORMULA

Overtime hours = number of hours worked in week – regular working hours

THE COMPONENTS

Overtime is the number of hours an employee spends in the workplace over and above the contracted working hours which, of course, vary according to the type of industry (software, auto-manufacturing and so on) and the level of the particular worker (unskilled laborer, engineer and so on) within the organization's hierarchy.

The variation in the overtime figure helps an organization to analyze seasonal changes in labor demand, the motivation of employees and the factors affecting these.

In calculating overtime hours, the company may also need to consider factors such as the general health and stress levels of employees, as well as their previous efficiency levels.

Penalty rates of pay may apply for staff working overtime beyond the standard contract of, say, 40 hours per week or outside the normal spread of hours on public holidays or other days that are not rostered for work.

WHERE'S THE DATA?

Overtime data can be gathered from automated or manual activity-tracker registers or from employees' time sheets. The use of automated systems such as swipe cards and biometric technologies can help streamline the process. The use of time-tracking systems that capture arrival time, leaving time and the time spent on different activities can also be used for project planning, cost analysis, workflow analysis and performance/productivity assessments.

CALCULATING IT — AN EXAMPLE

Consider the following case of a manufacturing organization, XYZ Co. The overtime for an employee is calculated in the following manner:

Contract hours	40 hours per week
Typical work roster	8am–5pm Monday to Friday, one hour for lunch
Actual work pattern	8am–5pm Monday to Wednesday 8am–6pm Thursday to Friday 8am to 12 noon Saturday
Actual hours worked	46 hours
Overtime hours worked	46 – 40 = 6 hours

WHAT IT MEANS

Overtime data collated over a period of time can provide a company with useful information regarding its workforce-planning processes. For example, an unusually high bill for overtime pay against industry norms may point to staffing or productivity problems which, in turn, may require a reassessment of employees' skills, management abilities and/or planning capabilities.

While high levels of overtime at a particular period may merely reflect seasonal variations in demand for the company's products, they may also indicate variations in workload or in the health, morale or stress levels across departments.

The measurement of overtime and its associated trends is vital for managing labor costs, for workforce planning and for gauging an organization's capacity to respond to fluctuations in demand.

7 The HR Budget as a Percentage of Sales

THE DEFINITION

The HR department within any organization is responsible for, amongst other things, developing effective recruitment and selection techniques; maintaining good labor and employee relations; formulating compensation packages; organizing measures to ensure the continuing health and well-being of the workforce; and developing effective HR development policies. HR staff are involved in a range of consultative, change-management and administrative roles.

Over the years, there have been great debates over how resources are allocated to HR departments and much has been written about the role of HR in responding to the changing demands of an increasingly knowledge-based economy. HR, too, is in transition, from its traditional operational role to one that requires it to be a strategic partner to business. Though the old personnel department acquired a new name to reflect its more strategic role in the 1980s, the HR function is still considered somewhat "fuzzy" because it deals with the soft side of the business. Unlike production, marketing, sales, and finance, the HR function is not considered one whose performance can be measured or quantified in dollar terms or as a business metric.

We are going to explore the relationship between the HR department's budget and the company's total sales. Admittedly, there can be no one figure that will fit for all companies; rather, the appropriate figure is based on the context within which the company operates. Globalization has affected HR budget allocations in accordance with how companies prioritize their business development needs.

THE FORMULA

For any given year, the basic formula can be stated as follows:

$$\text{HR budget as a percentage of sales} = \frac{\text{Total HR department budget}}{\text{Total sales of the company}} \times 100\%$$

THE COMPONENTS

The HR department budget can be broken into the following simple components:

- HR staff salaries and costs

- budgets for recruitment campaigns and the use of agencies

- budgets for training and development.

WHERE'S THE DATA?

The data on the HR budget can be found in the company's annual budget allocations made at the beginning of the year. The sales figures are in the company's income statement.

CALCULATING IT — AN EXAMPLE

Let's take the example of a cement company, "A", whose total sales are US$1.8 billion, with an operating profit ratio of 12% (the industry average). The company's total planned budget for its HR department is US$10 million. The calculation is as follows:

$$\text{HR budget as a percentage of sales} = \frac{\text{US\$10,000,000}}{\text{US\$1.8 billion}} \times 100\%$$
$$= 0.55\%$$

A similar calculation can also be done to determine the HR department's budget as a proportion of the company's operating costs, as follows:

$$\text{Operating costs} = \text{US\$1.8 billion} \times 88\%$$
$$= \text{US\$1.58 billion}$$

$$\text{HR budget as a proportion of operating costs} = \frac{\text{HR budget}}{\text{Operating costs}} \times 100\%$$

$$= \frac{\text{US\$10,000,000}}{\text{US\$1.58 billion}} \times 100\%$$

$$= 0.63\%$$

WHAT IT MEANS

An increase in the ratio can point to a number of things, one of which is that the role of the HR department within the organization is becoming more complex and might require greater analysis. But it may also indicate a need to review work practices or to investigate better technology or outsourcing options, or it may suggest that the department is over-staffed. A decrease in the ratio is typically regarded as a positive organizational outcome that may simply reflect how well the company is leveraging its HR resources across its workforce. Alternatively, it may be the result of improvements in work practices and technology such that fewer staff are required.

Using these industry averages, the company can keep track of how its HR policies (and budget) are affecting performance. It should search for benchmarks within the industry and should try to realign its costs with those of the industry's best practices.

HR Staff as a Percentage of Total Staff

THE DEFINITION

HR staff ratio refers to the number of HR staff as a proportion of the total number of employees within an organization. This is an important consideration for budget-planning purposes because it provides a measure of the efficiency of HR department operations.

THE FORMULA

$$\text{HR staff as a percentage of total staff} = \frac{\text{No. of HR staff}}{\text{Total no. of staff}} \times 100\%$$

THE COMPONENTS

The *HR staff* is taken to include both the workforce and the management who are involved in the company's HR activities.

Total number of staff is the sum total of all full-time equivalent staff employed by the organization in any given pay period.

WHERE'S THE DATA?

Data related to staff designation can be found within the HR department's own records. Some HR staff may be seconded to other departments for various administrative reasons and care needs to be taken to include all these members in the head count.

CALCULATING IT — AN EXAMPLE

Total no. of employees $= 2,300$
No. of HR staff $= 27$

$$\text{HR staff as a percentage of total staff} = \frac{27}{2,300} \times 100\%$$

$$= 1.17\%$$

WHAT IT MEANS

While this ratio varies from industry to industry, studies have shown that HR staff, on average, comprise 1% of the total staff in most organizations.

Even within an organization the ratio does not hold constant, tending to vary from 0.8% to 1.2% as companies readjust their staffing levels in line with changing industry conditions. Where smaller organizations experience a large shrinkage in the size of their workforce, a number of HR staff — albeit minimal — are still required to manage the core HR functions.

Surveys have revealed a wide variation in HR staff ratios across various industries. For instance, HR staffing remains comparatively light (0.8%) among employers in the "non-business" sector, particularly among hospitals and other health-care facilities. In contrast, higher staffing ratios (over 1.2%) are more common among industries in the services/non-manufacturing sector.

It has also been observed that the percentage of HR staff declines as the size of the organization increases. This is probably due to the effect of economies of scale.

There is no ideal HR staff ratio because of the effect of a number of factors such as the effectiveness of the existing HR capability, economies of scale, and the extent to which HR requirements are outsourced.

Common factors that typically lead to an increase in the number and ratio of the HR staff are:

- a need to focus on issues related to the development of professional and managerial employees

- a need to focus on managing relations with the trade unions within the company

- the complexity and diversity of the business

- a company-wide emphasis on HR

- a tendency to avoid using outside consultants and services

- a minimal use of information technology.

Thus management expectations, the context of the business planning, and productivity are all key factors in determining the optimal size of the HR staff.

There is an increasing trend towards outsourcing HR-related activities to specialist organizations. The activities outsourced include job-requirement analysis, the short-listing and selection of employees, testing, training and evaluation.

9

IT Staff as a Percentage of Total Staff

THE DEFINITION

IT staff as a percentage of total staff indicates the level of investment made by the organization in the IT function. This indicator also provides a benchmark against which to evaluate the efficiency and robustness of the organization's IT infrastructure.

THE FORMULA

IT staff as a percentage of total staff

$$= \frac{\text{No. of employees in IT roles}}{\text{Total no. of employees}} \times 100\%$$

THE COMPONENTS

A staffing ratio can be used as a benchmark for how well resources are being allocated and to gauge how well capacity is being utilized within the company. It is calculated by dividing the number of personnel in one function by the number in another, and expressing it as a ratio; for example, 10:1 or 10.

Personnel employed in IT roles are the employees (full-time and full-time equivalent) working directly under the direction of the information technology/systems department in an organization at a particular point of time.

Where's the Data?

The data for staff with IT roles can be gathered from the payroll system and/or the employees' files maintained within each department. The particular industry standards can be obtained from the Internet or HR consultant firms that conduct specific industry research.

Calculating it — an Example

A simple example will illustrate the calculation.

Department	Number of employees
Finance	120
Systems/IT	40
Marketing	280
Operations	260
Total	**700**

$$\text{IT staff ratio} = \frac{40}{700} \times 100\%$$
$$= 5.71\%$$

What it Means

An upward change in the ratio of IT staff typically indicates one of a number of situations:

The organization is investing more in creating technology to gain competitive advantage, reduce costs, improve efficiency, or achieve more rapid delivery of services. The impact of IT has reduced staffing levels in operational areas through using technology platforms to deliver services more cost-effectively. A high ratio of IT staff could also be a cause for concern, and may indicate inefficient work practices, delayed systems delivery, old technology platforms and overstaffing.

A downward trend in the IT staff ratio typically indicates the opposite, where cost-cutting is being undertaken, savings are being gained and the appetite for cutting-edge systems is no longer being pursued.

Marketing Staff as a Percentage of Total Staff

THE DEFINITION

This is the number of personnel employed in a marketing role as a percentage of total number of personnel employed in the entire organization and provides a measure of how important the marketing function is to the organization. The proportion is generally high for companies which introduce a range of innovative products into the market and where competition is very tough, and lower for manufacturing firms.

THE FORMULA

Marketing staff as a percentage of total staff

$$= \frac{\text{No. of employees in marketing roles}}{\text{Total no. of employees}} \times 100\%$$

THE COMPONENTS

Marketing is an organizational function and a set of processes for creating, communicating and delivering value to customers and for managing customer relationships in ways that benefit the organization and its stakeholders.

The marketing function includes people who are responsible for controlling and maintaining marketing activities such as advertising, selling and distribution, and brand promotion. Personnel employed in marketing roles are those employees (full-time and full-time equivalent) working directly under the control of the marketing function of the organization at a particular point of time.

WHERE'S THE DATA?

The data for the marketing department, and all other departments, can be gathered from the payroll system.

CALCULATING IT — AN EXAMPLE

Department	Number of employees
Finance	220
Marketing	200
Operations	180
Total	**600**

$$\text{Marketing staff ratio} = \frac{200}{600} \times 100\%$$
$$= 33.33\%$$

WHAT IT MEANS

Usually, this ratio is compared to the industry median or the median of a sample of similar companies. Sometimes comparisons are also made across industries to enable the organizations to learn from practices outside their industry. When choosing a peer group for comparison, always pick companies that have similar product lines or the comparison will not be meaningful.

A ratio higher than the industry's mean could imply a higher dependency on marketing personnel, though this may not necessarily be true in all cases. For example, a company may need a higher number of marketing personnel to provide it with a competitive advantage arising from the customer service, the product range or the innovation it offers.

The figures vary from industry to industry. For example, a company in the fast-moving consumer-goods industry typically would have a higher proportion of its staff engaged in marketing activities than, say, an automobile manufacturing firm.

The information provided by this "magic number" may also provide an organization with insights into its internal functions. For example, managing a brand requires a cross-functional group of people; calculating the percentage of marketing staff employed in that particular brand over a period of time will indicate trends in the company's management of different kinds of brands.

Having this information at hand will also be of use when it comes to allocating department budgets and in determining the efficiency of individual departments.

Payroll Staff as a Percentage of Total Staff

THE DEFINITION

The payroll process includes all activities required to pay the employees' salaries and wages in line with company policies and government regulations. These activities include monitoring each employee's time and attendance records, calculating and distributing pay, and ensuring compliance with applicable government regulations through withholding taxes and premiums and remitting them to the appropriate agencies.

In most companies, the payroll process is the responsibility of a designated payroll department or the payroll section of the HR department. Part of the payroll function is to maintain and update all payroll-related data, process payroll accounting entries and respond to payroll inquiries.

Companies that apply best practices in processing payroll seek to minimize payroll costs and maximize service to employees, within the constraints of company policy and government regulations.

THE FORMULA

Payroll staff as percentage of total staff

$$= \frac{\text{No. of staff in payroll-related activities}}{\text{Total no. of staff}} \times 100\%$$

THE COMPONENTS

Payroll staff refers to employees within an organization who are involved in payroll-processing activities.

Total number of staff is the sum total of all full-time and full-time equivalent staff employed by the organization in any given pay period.

WHERE'S THE DATA?

Data related to staff designation can be found in the records of the HR department.

CALCULATING IT — AN EXAMPLE

The following example illustrates this straightforward calculation.

Total no. of employees $= 1,000$
No. of staff members in payroll dept. $= 3$
Payroll staff as a percentage of total staff $= \dfrac{3}{1000} \times 100\%$
$= 0.3\%$

WHAT IT MEANS

The basic purpose of analyzing and measuring this factor is to monitor the expenses incurred in payroll activities, which must be kept at a cost-effective level. Increasingly, outsourcing or IT initiatives are also being taken in order to minimize payroll-related expenses because these expenses do not add any value to an organization.

Percentage of Employees Making Suggestions

THE DEFINITION

This is largely self-explanatory and is a measure of the level of interest employees have in working towards the improvement and efficient functioning of the organization.

THE FORMULA

$$\text{Percentage making suggestions} = \frac{\text{No. making suggestions}}{\text{Total number of employees}} \times 100\%$$

THE COMPONENTS

The *total number of employees* is the total number of full-time and full-time equivalent employees in the organization at a particular time.

Suggestions are the ideas, recommendations or proposals made towards improving the functioning of an organization — in a process, in cost-cutting, in seeking new business opportunity, in increasing sales or increasing the motivation of employees — and can be either written or oral.

This measure can be used to compare the involvement of employees within different departments or between organizations.

The suggestions may be evaluated by the appropriate line managers from various departments against a range of criteria, including feasibility, viability and the degree to which they are accepted by other employees.

WHERE'S THE DATA?

Many organizations keep records of all suggestions made by their employees and the necessary information can be obtained there.

CALCULATING IT — AN EXAMPLE

NAME	SUGGESTION	CLASSIFICATION	STATUS
Peter	Outstation checks should also be accepted as fees	Written	Under consideration
	Outsource the meeting hall operations	Oral	Rejected
	Entries in meeting hall register should be cross-checked to prevent discrepancies	Written	Implemented
Paul	Buy computers from Dell	Oral	Under consideration
	Have 10-member core committee in annual dinner and dance planning	Oral	Under consideration
Patrick	Recreation club should also include games like Scrabble and Carom	Written	Under consideration
	Introduce one-day-per-year community volunteer work for staff	Oral	Rejected
Total = 3			

Records such as this keep account of both the number of suggestions and the number of employees who make them. In the above example, three employees have made suggestions. Let's say for the sake of illustration that the company has 30 employees. Thus, 10% of the staff have submitted suggestions, either in written or oral form.

WHAT IT MEANS

This measure gives an indication of the degree of involvement that the employees have in the organization. It can also reveal whether employees in particular departments are more involved than others. A high degree of involvement from employees might tend to suggest good relations between the employer and staff.

The figures revealed by this measure can be benchmarked against the experience of other, similar, organizations. Where the percentage is lower than the industry norm, this might suggest that the company needs to examine ways to encourage greater involvement from its workforce.

13

Process–cycle Time

THE DEFINITION

Process-cycle time is the time taken to complete a process from initiation to completion.

THE FORMULA

Process-cycle time = Process-initiation time
+ Processing time
+ Waiting time between the various sub-processes
+ Implementation time

THE COMPONENTS

Process-initiation time is the time taken to set a process into action.

Processing time is the time required to execute the various steps required.

Waiting time between the various sub-processes is the time that elapses from the completion of one activity in the sequence to the beginning of the next.

Implementation time is the time taken from the completion of the process to the time the service is made available for use.

The costs involved with this process are those associated with the HR department's ability to provide the required service efficiently. This, in turn, depends on the degree to which roles and responsibilities are clearly defined and assigned. There may be other costs associated with the need to re-allocate work within the department and with the adequacy of the technology allocated for undertaking the task. Where inadequacies in the process lead to fragmented functions or a replication of activities or require staff to work overtime to complete their assigned tasks, these costs will obviously be higher.

WHERE'S THE DATA?

All of the components outlined above can be estimated from the documentation relating to the process or, where the organization maintains an information system, from the central database. The estimates of the waiting time can also be gauged from past experience.

The process-cycle time for getting leave sanctioned in an organization with self-administered systems is usually determined by the automated leave-processing system maintained on software such as PeopleSoft, as outlined below.

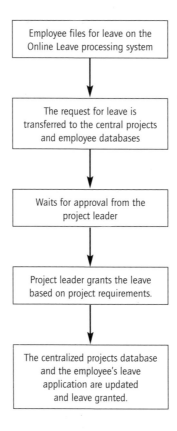

CALCULATING IT — AN EXAMPLE

Let us assume that an employee applies for leave on the morning of Monday the 15th of the month for leave on Friday the 19th. As soon as the employee files the request, the project leader immediately receives notification of this from the automated leave-processing system. The centralized projects database is also updated immediately. The project leader checks for possible clashes with the project schedules during the requested leave period. Where there is a potential clash, the leader may be able to allocate other resources, in which case the request can be approved. Where there are no clashes, the leave application is processed directly and the projects database and the leave-application system are updated accordingly. The entire cycle may take half an hour to a couple of hours to complete and varies according to such things as the availability of the project leader or resource-allocation constraints.

WHAT IT MEANS

A low process-cycle time relative to the industry norm is an indication of the efficiency of the internal function and the HR staff who administer it.

Cycle times can be decreased through the increased use of technology to improve speed and quality of service. This leads to greater customer satisfaction and managers gain extra confidence that they can rely on the HR department to deliver efficient and effective services to the business.

Profit Per Employee

THE DEFINITION

Profit per employee is a measure applied to determine an organization's productivity at the level of the individual employee. It is defined as operating profit per employee, taking into account all full-time, casual and part-time employees of the company.

The profit-per-employee figure provides a broad indication of how much it costs to run a company. It can be particularly useful when measuring the efficiency of businesses.

THE FORMULA

$$\text{Profit per employee} = \frac{\text{Operating profit}}{\text{No. of full-time equivalent employees}}$$

THE COMPONENTS

- *Full-time equivalent employees* refers to the total of employees working 40 hours per week (or the normal working week as defined by a country's laws). This includes part-time and casual workers, whose hours are converted to their full-time equivalents, and the hours of overtime worked by full-time employees. Profit per employee may vary across departments and hierarchy levels.

The employees may be classified as skilled/unskilled; as managerial/operations/support staff; or according to department/function (for example, marketing, human resources, operations).

WHERE'S THE DATA?

The data for the net profit can be obtained from the company's financial statements.

The data for calculating full-time equivalent employee figures can be obtained from the payroll system or employees' data sheets.

CALCULATING IT — AN EXAMPLE

Let's say, for example, that the operating profit for XYZ Co. is $1 million. The data obtained from the company's records is as follows:

No. of full-time employees:	350
No. of overtime hours per eight-hour working day per full-time employee:	1
Therefore, equivalent FTEs (overtime):	$\dfrac{1 \times 350}{8}$
	$= 43.75$
No. of part-time employees:	100 which equates to:
Equivalent FTEs (part-time):	50
Total no. of FTEs:	$350 + 50 + 43.75$
	$= 443.75$
Profit per employee	$= \dfrac{\$1 \text{ million}}{443.75}$
	$= \$2,253.52$

WHAT IT MEANS

Companies with profit-per-employee figures greater than the industry average are generally considered more efficient than those with lower figures. A higher profit-per-employee figure indicates that the company can operate on low overhead costs and, therefore, do more with fewer employees, which often translates into healthy profits.

The profit-per-employee figure is best used to compare similar companies rather than across industries. Retailers and other service-oriented companies that employ a lot of people, for instance, will have dramatically different ratios from those of software firms.

Early-stage businesses typically have low profit-per-employee figures, particularly those involved in developing new technology.

15 Response Time Per Request for Information

THE DEFINITION

Response time per request for information is the time it takes to provide employee-specific information (for example, payroll data or superannuation/medical benefit details) when requested. It is measured using the response-time metric outlined below.

THE FORMULA

Transaction response time = Time of completion – Time of receipt

THE COMPONENTS

Time of completion (TC) is the time at which the complete information requested is made available to the requester, either on paper or in electronic form.

Time of receipt (TR) is the time at which a request for information is submitted to the appropriate department, either on paper or in electronic form.

The time period between TR and TC can be broken down into the following sub-components which will determine the total transaction time of the system:

Time Component	Description
Validation time	Time required to validate the credentials of the requester where access to privileged information is requested
Search time	Time required to search for the desired information
Processing and presentation time	Time required to consolidate and present the information in the desired format

WHERE'S THE DATA?

The recording methods used will vary from company to company. Where manual or semi-automated systems are used, the request and completion information will be recorded by a member of the administrative staff.

Other companies may operate a fully automated system in which the transaction processing rate is a function of the technology, system architecture, hardware and software components used.

Access to such information is easily obtained by those authorized to do so.

CALCULATING IT — AN EXAMPLE

Suppose an employee files a request for a duplicate copy of his last month's salary slip. He files his request on the first day of the week, within the first hour of his working day. The entire process of filing the request and receiving an acknowledgement note from the administrative unit takes half an hour and is completed by 9.30 am.

He finally receives the requested salary slip at the end of his eight-hour shift at 5.00pm.

Then

Time of receipt   = 9.30 am
Time of completion   = 5.00 pm
Transaction response time = 7.5 hours

Where responses take more than one day, the metric can either add a standard eight hours for each working day or denominate the number of working days between the time of receipt and time of completion.

WHAT IT MEANS

Response time is an important determinant of both the efficiency of the department providing the information and the quality of service as perceived by the organization's employees. In many organizations, the use of technology and smart systems has led to a substantial reduction in typical transaction-response rates, leading to more satisfied customers and HR staff and to better deployment of resources on higher-value work.

A low response time increases the organization's overall productivity by reducing the time employees spend on activities not directly linked to business results. A high response time is indicative of the need for improvements in work-flows and procedures associated with the information request-and-retrieval process.

Whether the system employed is entirely manual or fully automated, response time can be used as a criterion for evaluating its efficiency. Excellent response times provide staff with confidence in the HR system and the capability of the HR department. At the same time, managers are assured that the HR department is operating efficiently and may be relied on to support other business initiatives.

Many organizations negotiate a "service standard" for each class of common queries and track the performance of the HR department on these measures. Tracking the response rates along with seasonal trends can also help HR managers in the scheduling of staff at critical times. For example, it may be necessary to schedule extra staff to meet the service standards at peak times associated with pay day, public and religious holidays, or the influx of seasonal staff. In many cases, the "service standard" has a tolerance factor to allow for difficult cases, unforeseen difficulties and sudden shifts in demand — for example, "respond to pay queries within eight hours, 95% of the time".

16

Sick-leave Rate

THE DEFINITION

Sick leave can be taken by an employee when he/she is sick or injured, or when the employee's spouse or a dependent person (such as a child or elderly parent) is sick or injured and needs care. Individual sick-leave entitlements are determined by the employee's working status; that is, whether permanent full-time, permanent part-time, casual full-time or casual part-time. Different sick-leave rates could occur in different sub-groups of an organization's workforce and these need to be considered while calculating sick-leave rates.

The *sick-leave rate* is the number of employees in an organization who take sick leave within a specified period as a proportion of the total workforce within that organization. This can be broken down into various sub-groups (middle-level managers, shop-floor employees, interns, business units and so on) as required.

THE FORMULA

$$\text{Sick-leave rate} = \frac{\text{No. of staff taking sick leave}}{\text{Total no. of staff}}$$

THE COMPONENTS

The rate can be calculated by category of employee because rates differ from category to category, depending on environment, work arrangements and so on. Having this information enables comparisons to be made across categories, environment, and work arrangements.

WHERE'S THE DATA?

Sick-leave data is typically recorded in the leave log of individual employees, which is generally available in the payroll system.

CALCULATING IT — AN EXAMPLE

Let us take as an example calculating the sick-leave rate among junior-level managers in a particular month:

No. of junior-level managers $= 84$
Emergency sick leave $= 7$ days
Pre-arranged sick leave $= 8$ days
Total $= 15$ days
Sick-leave rate $= \dfrac{15}{84} = 0.179$ or 17.9%

Sick leave needs to be measured at a sub-group level to indicate the trend for the group.

Other detailed analysis can be conducted to break down the information still further to measure areas such as:

- the number of paid sick-leave days per employee

- the number of unpaid sick-leave days per employee

- the incidence and frequency of lost time

- the average time lost

- the total sick-leave rate.

WHAT IT MEANS

High sick-leave rates, particularly when analyzed by sub-group or trends over time, can provide powerful indicators of serious occupational health issues and hazards with potentially severe consequences in the form of increased business costs, litigation, inspections from regulatory authorities, continuity of business and difficulties in operational management. They can be pointers, too, to general organizational dysfunction, resulting in poor morale, low productivity and absenteeism. Indeed, poor management of staffing practices may lead to inappropriate use of sick-leave entitlements by certain staff members.

Sick Days Per Full-time Equivalent Employee Per Year

THE DEFINITION

The number of sick days per full-time equivalent (FTE) employee per year is a measure of lost productivity. Analyzing this metric sheds light on patterns of sick-leave utilization, frequency of utilization and trends. The utilization pattern of sick leave can vary across industries and this can provide pointers for policy on sick leave.

THE FORMULA

$$\text{Sick days per FTE per year} = \frac{\text{Total no. of sick days in the reporting period}}{\text{Total no. of full-time equivalent employees}} \times 100\%$$

THE COMPONENTS

Sick leave is defined as number of days of paid or unpaid absence from work because of illness or injury that does not affect the contract of employment.

Full-time equivalent employees refers to the number of employees working the normal working hours, typically a 40-hour week. This, of course, differs by country in accordance with the statutory rules governing that country's work hours. This calculation also includes the full-time equivalent of all part-time and casual workers. *Per year* is defined as the total number of days for which full-time employees or full-time equivalent employees are contracted for or scheduled to work per year.

The extent to which sick leave is taken may be affected by workforce demographics such as diversity of age, education, salary levels and gender.

WHERE'S THE DATA?

The company's basic information systems will record such details as the precise number of sick days taken by employees and the full-time equivalent days per year.

Many companies maintain health files for their employees which may help throw light on the reasons behind a particular extended absence, if such information is required.

CALCULATING IT — AN EXAMPLE

Assuming the total number of days of sick leave taken by employees in a company is 30 and the number of full-time equivalent employees in that company is 300, then the sick days per full-time equivalent per year can be calculated as follows:

$$\text{Sick days per full-time equivalent per year} = \frac{30}{300} \times 100\%$$
$$= 10\%$$

WHAT IT MEANS

There is no ideal level at which this sick-leave rate should be, although many organizations now realize that trying to minimize sick leave can be ineffective. High levels of sick-leave utilization might be indicative of unsuitable working conditions, high stress at work, an unhealthy physical work environment and so on.

This is not to be regarded as a policing tool but as an effective tool that might help HR professionals and businesses to manage productivity and other workforce issues. Absence from work and the associated health-care costs and lost productivity can seriously affect the profitability of an organization and its capacity to deliver services to its customers.

Monitoring such trends enables an organization to identify potential problems in the workplace and areas that are not functioning efficiently and help develop a productive and happy workplace.

The Cost of Medical Disbursement by Category of Ailment

THE DEFINITION

This is a measure of the amount of money spent on employees' medical expenses for the treatment of particular ailments and expressed as a percentage of the company's overall expenditure on medical expenses.

The calculation would take into account such things as cash reimbursements or the costs involved in introducing preventative measures undertaken for the benefit of employees. More often than not, companies provide insurance to employees and their dependents to cover their medical expenditures and then reimburse them according to the claims filed.

THE FORMULA

Cost of medical disbursement by category of ailment

$$= \frac{\text{Medical expenses on particular ailment}}{\text{Total medical expenditure}}$$

THE COMPONENTS

Medical expenses on particular ailments include amounts reimbursed to employees for the expenses incurred to treat ailments (reimbursements for uninsured health or accident expenses) as well as for any money spent on undertaking preventative measures for such ailments.

Total medical expenditure includes the amount spent by the organization for all medical purposes. This also includes health insurance premiums paid by the company, even though they may not relate to any specific ailment. This should also include the amount spent on health promotion and wellness programs.

Cash reimbursements pertain to money paid to employees to cover their expenses on hospital bills, treatment charges, medicines and travel costs (where, for example, treatment is only available in a different city).

The above expenditures are usually calculated annually, although calculations based on quarterly or monthly data can also be evaluated.

WHERE'S THE DATA?

- Insurance claims filed by employees

- Employees' medical records maintained by the organization

- Bills for medical expenses supplied by employees

- The company's financial statements.

CALCULATING IT — AN EXAMPLE

In calculating the amount spent by the company on asthma, for example, the following would have to be considered:

---

1. Doctors' fees (consultation and treatment)
2. Diagnostic tests
3. Diagnostic scans
4. Medicine obtained by employees for treating ailment
5. Inhalers or other devices required to assist in breathing
6. Transportation expenses incurred if treatment to be obtained elsewhere
7. Expenses incurred on emergency operations or any surgical procedures
8. Routine care
9. Therapy benefits*
10. Total

(*Some companies also cover therapy benefits up to a certain amount on such things as homeopathy, stress-management workshops, dietary services, psychiatric treatment, and so on.)

When these costs have been calculated, this figure is then divided by the company's total medical expenditure to obtain the ratio for the specific ailment.

WHAT IT MEANS

- Analysis of the ratio calculated above would indicate clearly to the company, which ailment or disease was responsible for the largest proportion of its medical expenditure. This could perhaps throw light on the work environment by highlighting occupational hazards (where, for example, a large proportion of these expenses was incurred reimbursing employees for an illness caused by poor working conditions or hygiene factors) and pointing the company towards necessary improvements.

- The ratio could be compared to the industry average to see how the company's experience of particular ailments matches up with those of its peers. If it finds, for example, that its expenditure on diseases arising from unhealthy lifestyles (including smoking, lack of exercise or obesity) is higher than the norm, it could redesign its recruitment policies in such a way that it can select employees who do not present too many health risks for the company. It could also introduce programs designed to improve the health habits of existing employees and thus save on medical costs in the long term. For example, an evaluation of the financial and health impact of a large-scale corporate health and wellness program conducted for a large, fast-moving, consumer-goods company operating in Asia has shown that participating employees have significantly lower medical expenses and achieve overall health benefits in risk categories such as high cholesterol, hypertension and smoking.

- A company could also put a ceiling on the maximum amount it will reimburse for a particular disease. Thus, if asthma is accounting for a significant proportion of overall medical costs it could, for the sake of decreasing costs, reimburse only up to a predetermined amount for this illness.

Thus, keeping track of the costs of medical disbursement by category of ailment can be an effective measure for a company looking to reduce costs or to increase the well-being of its employees.

19 Time Taken to Fill a Job Vacancy

THE DEFINITION

This measures the average number of days it takes for an organization to hire a candidate for a job, from the day the job becomes available. Within an organization, this is taken to be the day on which a specific opening is recognized. From an external viewpoint, the vacancy is taken to be available from the day on which it is advertised by the company's HR department.

This is a key staffing performance measure and gives hiring managers an indication of how long it will take to fill vacant positions. Its value, like any human-capital metric, is in setting a benchmark against which the company is able to evaluate the extent to which it has achieved its goals and objectives, and how well it is performing vis-à-vis industry standards as a whole.

THE FORMULA

$$\text{Time to fill a job vacancy} = \frac{\text{Total no. of days required to fill vacancies}}{\text{Number hired}}$$

THE COMPONENTS

Total number of days required to fill vacancies is the number of days it took to fill every vacancy during a particular period.

The time taken to fill any position that becomes available could incorporate the time it takes to inform the HR department once the need is recognized; the time it takes to advertise the vacancy in newspapers or on the corporate website; the time allowed for potential candidates to submit their applications; the time spent in developing a rating plan, in rating and ranking applicants and in preparing a list of the best qualified; the time required for interviewing candidates; the time required for obtaining higher-level approval of the proposed candidate; the time required to undertake any necessary background investigation; and the time spent in notifying the selected candidate and in the candidate accepting the offer.

Number hired refers to the number of people hired during the specified time period, which is usually taken to be a year, although monthly or quarterly data can also be analyzed. Comparison across different departments or business units can be useful.

The costs associated with an unfilled position can be ascertained by calculating the average revenue generated in a day by an employee with an equivalent role and multiplying by the average number of days required to fill a vacancy.

WHERE'S THE DATA?

Where a position has become vacant following a resignation or dismissal, the company's personnel records will show the dates on which the post became vacant and when it was filled. Where a new position has been created, the minutes of the meeting at which the need was first discussed will be of help and the HR department's own records will show when the vacancy was filled.

The number of people hired in any particular period will be recorded in the payroll system.

CALCULATING IT — AN EXAMPLE

The calculation may look something like this:

Components	Avg No. of Calendar Days
Getting approval to fill a vacancy	2
Deciding on the appropriate recruitment campaign	1
Launching the campaign	1
Developing a rating plan	1
Rating and ranking applicants & preparing the best-qualified lists	2
Interviewing candidates	3
Making the final selection	1
Obtaining higher-level approval of the proposed candidate	11
Completing required background investigations	20
Notifying the selected person and obtaining acceptance of job offer	3
Total no. of days elapsed to fill the vacancy	**45**

WHAT IT MEANS

If the time taken to fill a vacancy is higher than the industry standard, this can have a number of adverse effects on the organization, as outlined below. Further departmental comparisons can help determine which units are taking longer for the process of filling vacancies.

Product development and productivity

The time it takes to get a product to market is influenced by every link in the production chain. Because inter-departmental schedules and plans are closely interwoven, any disruption in one department may have adverse effects in all others.

In industries that are subject to seasonal variations in demand, any disruption may be even more costly. Unduly long delays in filling vacancies in key skilled positions may mean that products and projects have to be dropped altogether.

Impact on team

The progress of products that are dependent on teams for their development may be severely affected by the lost productivity, experience, leadership, ideas and skills that accompany a long delay in filling a key vacancy.

Longer vacancies may exert pressure on other employees who may be asked to do extra work until the vacancy is filled. This may lead to an increase in the number of accidents or errors, resulting in a lowering of product quality.

Impact on individual employees

A vacancy within a department often requires that someone else do the work until it is filled. That person may not be familiar with the role and this can lead to a lowering of productivity.

Where departments are understaffed, it is less likely that staff will be able to attend training courses or conferences, which may lead to increased stress or frustration.

If temps are hired in the interim, they usually have a higher error rate than the average employee and they are unlikely to generate many new ideas.

Increased management time and effort

Where a position is vacant for a long period, managers often have to skip their normal planning and responsibilities in order to fill in for the unfilled position.

If the vacancies are caused by top management decisions (budget freezes, for example) it can cause managers to lose hope. This can affect morale and may lead to a high management turnover rate.

Loss of competitive advantage

Where vacancies remain unfilled for an extended period, this may lead to a position where less-suitable candidates are employed, making it more difficult to hire any new top performers later on.

Part TWO

MAGIC NUMBERS FOR STAFFING AND LEARNING

MAGIC NUMBERS FOR STAFFING AND LEARNING

In this section we look at the metrics used to measure staffing activities and learning efforts within organizations. These are covered in the following "magic numbers":

20. Staff-turnover cost by recruitment source

21. Employee-engagement index

22. Involuntary staff-turnover rate

23. Turnover rate by job category and job performance

24. Voluntary staff-turnover rate

25. Competency-development expense per employee

26. Training hours per employee

27. Cost per trainee hour

28. Percentage of employees trained, by category

20 Staff-turnover Cost by Recruitment Source

THE DEFINITION

Capturing turnover costs by recruitment source enables comparisons to be made across recruitment sources. This metric has two components. One is the proportionate costs incurred in the recruiting and hiring process for prospective employees who received job offers but chose not to join. The other is costs incurred in the form of training, wages and benefits given to those employees who are recruited through a particular recruiting source but leave the organization within the appraisal period.

THE FORMULA

Cost of turnover by recuitment source $=$

$$\left(\frac{\text{Declined offers}}{\text{Total no. of offers made}}\right) \times (\text{Recruiting costs})$$

$$+ \left[\left(\frac{\text{No. of employees leaving within three months}}{\text{Total no. of offers made}}\right)\right.$$

$$\left. \times (\text{Hiring costs} + \text{Training costs} + \text{Wages \& benefits})\right]$$

$$+ \text{Replacement-time costs}$$

THE COMPONENTS

Total no. of offers made is the number of offers made by the organization to prospective employees during the recruitment and hiring process.

Declined offers refers to the number of prospective employees who do not respond and/or reject the offers, within the prescribed time limit.

Recruiting costs will be the total amount spent on:

- finding job applicants by way of advertisement, references, etc

- reviewing applications and screening process

- traveling and accommodation expenses (own and candidates', if reimbursed)

- costs of preparing offer and legal documents

- third-party commission charges, if applicable

- any other direct expenses.

No. of employees leaving is the number of employees who join the organization but leave within the appraisal period, thus obliging the company to repeat the process.

Hiring costs will include the value of various equipment provided (car, personal computer, and so on), and the travel expenses (own and candidates') incurred in finalizing the agreements.

Training costs include direct expenses incurred on induction and initial training, relocation charges, management time and reduced-productivity costs, and travel expenditures incurred during training.

Wages and benefits costs include salary and benefits given during the appraisal period.

Replacement-time costs are the costs incurred until suitable candidates are found to fill vacancies. They consist of HR services and costs, loss-of-revenue costs, and legal costs and severance expenses.

WHERE'S THE DATA?

The data regarding the number of offers made and the offers rejected and various financial details regarding the total recruiting expenses can be found within the HR department and/or the recruitment agency, depending on company processes.

Details of hiring and training costs and wages and benefits should be available within the company's payroll system. Some organizations maintain a separate system for employees under appraisal, thus facilitating data collection and application.

CALCULATING IT — AN EXAMPLE

During the recruitment process, assume that 100 of the candidates who applied for the job are given final offers to join the company. If only 80 of these finally join the company, we have 20 rejections from the final call-list. The costs incurred in dealings with these 20 candidates are included in turnover costs.

In this case, the costs for recruiting are as follows:

Advertising	$2,000
Reviewing applications/screening process	$7,000
Travel and accommodation expenses	$10,000
Preparing offer and legal documents	$4,500
Third-party commission charges	$1,500
Total recruiting costs	$25,000

The costs incurred on the 20 declined offers would be:

$$\frac{\text{Declined offers}}{\text{Total no. of offers made}} \times \text{Recruiting costs}$$

$$= \frac{20}{100} \times \text{recruiting costs}$$

$$= \frac{20}{100} \times 25,000$$

$$= \$5,000$$

Let's assume that the company's appraisal period is three months. After this, 10 of the 80 recruits leave the company. Now, the cost incurred in recruiting these people is added to the turnover costs.

During the appraisal period, the various costs that are incurred are as follows:

Hiring costs:

Value of equipment provided	$10,000

Training costs:

Travel expenses	$50,000
Material expenses	$45,000

Wages & benefits costs:

Salary and benefits given	$300,000
Ongoing non-productivity costs	$15,000

Total costs incurred during appraisal period are $420,000

Turnover costs incurred as a result of the 10 people leaving are as follows:

$$\left[\left(\frac{\text{No. of employees leaving}}{\text{Total no. of offers made}} \right) \right.$$
$$\left. \times \ (\text{Hiring costs} + \text{Training costs} + \text{Wages \& benefits}) \right]$$
$$= \frac{10}{100} \times 420,000 = \$42,000$$

However, there are other costs to be considered as a result of these people leaving after the appraisal period. These are the costs incurred until replacements can be found.

Replacement-time costs include:

HR services & costs	$10,000
Legal costs	$20,000
Severance payments	$15,000
Total	$45,000

Hence, the total turnover cost by recruitment source in our example is thus:

$$\frac{\text{Declined offers}}{\text{Total no. of offers made}} \times \text{Recruiting costs}$$

$$+ \left[\left(\frac{\text{No. of employees leaving}}{\text{Total no. of offers made}} \right) \right.$$

$$\left. \times (\text{Hiring costs} + \text{Training costs} + \text{Wages \& benefits}) \right]$$

$$+ \text{Replacement-time costs}$$

$$= \$(5,000 + 42,000 + 45,000) = \$92,000$$

WHAT IT MEANS

We can calculate the turnover costs for the recruitment process from the different recruitment agencies currently being used by the company and compare their respective cost-efficiency.

Very high turnover costs may be a pointer to problems in the recruitment process and should alert the company to the need to look for an alternative, more efficient source.

21 Employee-engagement Index

THE DEFINITION

The employee-engagement index (EEI) is based on periodic surveys conducted to gauge the opinions of employees. The EEI is a valuable tool in that it allows management to keep abreast of the most compelling issues facing their employees and hence creates a call to action. In addition, it provides a focus on the issues that truly make a difference to the efficiency of an organization, and helps management make effective use of its employees' skills.

THE FORMULA

$$EEI = \frac{No.\ of\ satisfied\ employees}{No.\ of\ staff\ responding\ to\ survey} \times 100\%$$

THE COMPONENTS

The survey typically uses a series of questions for which the responses are rated against a five-point Likert scale — Strongly Agree, Agree, Neither Agree nor Disagree, Disagree, and Strongly Disagree. From this, the degree of engagement or disengagement can be assessed for each question and key theme.

The engagement index is derived from the percentage of satisfied employees responding to the survey. It can also be useful to establish the percentage of staff who have neutral views on any subject. Management can take appropriate measures to address areas of concern when the survey reflects that there is a high percentage of discontent. All the values in the index help provide a balanced picture of staff engagement on topics covered in the survey.

The survey results can help the organization identify its unique areas of strength and areas of genuine concern vis-à-vis industry norms.

However, even with norm comparisons, managers may have trouble in identifying the areas for follow-up that are likely to have the greatest impact on organizational performance. They then have to explore any possible connections between the survey findings and the organization's results.

It should be clear from the survey results which issues engage employees most and which have least impact. The organization can then focus its activities accordingly. It helps, too, to be able to measure changes in engagement that may become obvious from one survey to the next or over a series of such surveys. This approach is illustrated in Figure 1.

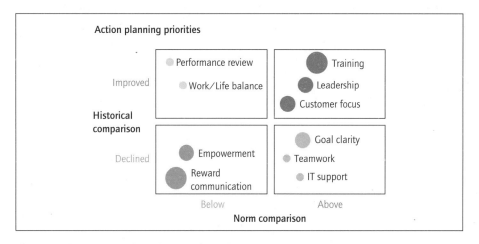

Figure 1   Focusing on key drivers of employee engagement

The size of the circle indicates the strength of the key-driver effect (the larger the circle, the stronger the key driver). The upper right-hand quadrant represents the true strengths of the organization and should continue to be leveraged. Scores in this quadrant have improved; are above the norm and are significant key drivers of commitment. Scores in the bottom left-hand quadrant represent high-risk areas for which investments in follow-up action will have the greatest return.

Scores in these areas have declined; are below the norm and are key drivers of commitment.

In this example, the priorities for follow-up action should be the areas of empowerment (where staff are given autonomy to introduce solutions to what they see as problems) and reward communication (how the organization communicates its reward philosophy and policy to employees) — scores are below norm and have declined, and both issues are key drivers of employee commitment. In contrast, the area of training is a strength to be leveraged — scores are above norm, have improved and this area is also a key driver of commitment.

This approach allows managers to identify both the genuine areas of concern and the key drivers that will ultimately affect the organization's performance. Thus the organization can focus on the *vital few* issues that will have the greatest potential return on investment.

Also, important patterns can emerge from an examination of differences by divisions/business units, gender, age, location, and different types of jobs within a function or division. It is common for different groups of people to have different attitudes to questions — some groups are more optimistic or pessimistic than others. For example, sales, marketing and HR people could be more positive about the company's prospects than their colleagues in manufacturing or IT because they often have knowledge about sales figures and marketing success stories. Female employees are generally more positive than male employees; and job satisfaction tends to increase with more senior job levels. Again, normative comparisons with groups displaying the same characteristics can help put responses into perspective. In general, emerging markets are more positive than mature markets. For example, survey results tend to be much more positive in India than in Japan.

Where's the Data?

Data is gathered by using structured questions administered as either a printed or online survey. Questions are grouped around key topics that can include such things as compensation/benefits, working conditions, performance management, communication, teamwork, customer focus, leadership, supervision, tools/resources/training, organizational effectiveness, diversity and by job functions.

The survey data can be linked to other measures of organizational performance, such as customer satisfaction and financial performance. This has become well established in research published in 1997 in the *The Service-Profit Chain*, by James L. Heskett, W. Earl Sasser and Leonard A. Schlesinger, where it was found that employee engagement leads to customer satisfaction and this, in turn, leads to superior business performance. However, the key drivers of employee engagement will vary by culture, industry sector and organizational context. A one-size-fits-all approach is likely to miss the key driver that will have the greatest impact on long-term performance. Figure 2 below illustrates the factors affecting employee engagement and the link to an organization's performance.

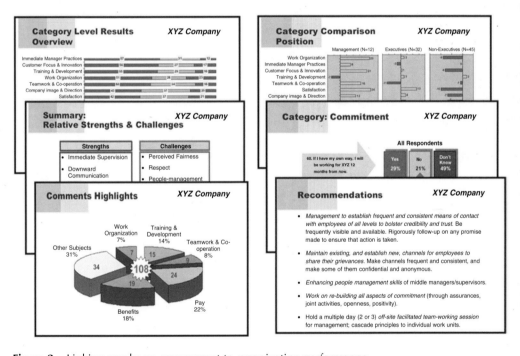

Figure 2   Linking employee engagement to organization performance

CALCULATING IT

To calculate an EEI, a scale can be designed to measure the responses, from "highly dissatisfied" to "highly satisfied" and the percentage score for each category can be calculated.

WHAT IT MEANS

Ratings, rankings, comparisons and trends over time provide a clear indication of the past actions that have helped create the prevailing mood in the organization. They identify the key themes and issues that specific groups or populations at large deem to be in need of management attention, and the key drivers of commitment that cause productivity to drop and staff turnover to increase. These results provide an opportunity to improve business performance across the organization.

22 Involuntary Staff-turnover Rate

THE DEFINITION

Involuntary turnover happens when an employee is discharged or has his/her duties terminated by the organization. This typically happens when organizations have identified that the particular employee is unable to perform the duties required, no longer meets performance criteria, is guilty of gross and willful misconduct or is no longer required to meet operational needs.

Involuntary turnover also includes the frustration of a contract through death or permanent disability, as well as layoffs, retrenchment, redundancy and resignations in anticipation of dismissal.

THE FORMULA

$$\text{Involuntary turnover rate} = \frac{\text{Dismissals} + \text{Disability retirements} + \text{Layoffs}}{\text{Total no. of employees (period average)}}$$

CALCULATING IT — AN EXAMPLE

Average no. of employees during the period : 250
No. of dismissals : 3
No. of retirements through disability : 4
No. of layoffs : 10

$$\text{Involuntary turnover rate} = \frac{(3 + 4 + 10)}{250} \times 100\%$$
$$= 6.8\%$$

THE COMPONENTS

Dismissals are typically initiated for reasons of poor performance, gross and willful misconduct (such as theft), poor attendance or insubordination.

Disability retirement is typically initiated when there is frustration of the contract as a result of illness, injury and an inability to perform the duties of the job to the required standard.

Layoffs are typically invoked where there is insufficient work, where a financial or production downturn requires changes in staffing levels, technology changes make certain skills redundant or where the business changes location.

WHERE'S THE DATA?

Turnover data and the reasons for turnover are normally available from HR department records.

WHAT IT MEANS

An analysis of involuntary-turnover data creates the opportunity to identify the leading causes and to re-examine the organization's staff selection and planning processes. It can also raise questions as to whether there is a need to improve the performance management process and the supervisory skills of managers.

Depending on the business needs and culture of the organization, a low involuntary-turnover rate may be either a cause for celebration or for concern. The involuntary-turnover rate could be used with other accompanying metrics to derive a view about performance or productivity issues.

Turnover Rate by Job Category and Job Performance

THE DEFINITION

This metric measures how many permanent, full-time workers left the company and had to be replaced in a given period relative to the average number of workers employed at such workers' jobs and at equivalent performance levels.

THE FORMULA

$$\text{Turnover rate} = \frac{ES_{G,P}}{AE_{G,P}}$$

THE COMPONENTS

$ES_{G,P}$ is the number of employees of a particular grade (G) and performance level (P) who have left the organization.

$AE_{G,P}$ is the average number of employees working in that particular grade (G) and exhibiting the performance level (P).

Grade represents the job category to which a particular employee belongs. (For example, in a software organization, an engineer might fall into the trainee engineer, software engineer or senior software engineer category.)

Performance level represents the performance rating received in the most recent appraisal process.

WHERE'S THE DATA?

This data is available from the organization's performance-management system.

CALCULATING IT — AN EXAMPLE

The HR records of ABC Software Systems Ltd show that 10 of the 20 senior software engineers who were rated as having a performance level of 4 (that is, at the high end on a scale of 1 to 5) left the company between June 2003 and June 2004 — a turnover rate of 50%.

WHAT IT MEANS

HR typically tracks turnover of employees. But the added dimension of tracking turnover rate by job category as well as performance levels enables the organization to design and conduct specific retention and training programs based on the details available. HR can then use this information on the quality and grade of personnel moving out of the organization to help in its recruitment.

An organization will also be able to draw conclusions regarding possible links between job category/performance levels and the turnover rate. Essentially, organizations would need to address situations where consistent high performers leave the organization.

24 Voluntary Staff-turnover Rate

THE DEFINITION

Staff turnover has become a major concern for organizations today, with labor shortages and competitive pressures making retention a key issue. Given that its workforce is a primary determinant of an organization's performance, it stands to reason that an increase in staff turnover will have a detrimental effect on productivity. A great deal of attention is therefore given to the reasons why employees leave organizations of their own accord. This voluntary turnover, as it is called, can be influenced by any number of factors relating to individual circumstances, conditions within the company, industry trends and the general economic climate.

THE FORMULA

$$\text{Voluntary staff-turnover rate} = \frac{\text{No. of staff leaving voluntarily}}{\substack{\text{Total no. of employees} \\ \text{(period average)}}}$$

THE COMPONENTS

Within the voluntary turnover category there is what is referred to as "wanted" and "unwanted" turnover.

Wanted turnover covers those employees whom the organization doesn't mind losing, even if it means incurring replacement costs.

Unwanted turnover refers to the loss of those employees whom the organization would like keep. This category can be further broken down into the loss of a newcomer or the loss of a valued senior employee.

In the former case, turnover occurs within the first year of employment and, in an early-departure scenario, the bulk of the costs are replacement costs and initial training costs.

The latter case represents costs that are greater than simple replacement costs. The costs of losing a good performer are greater than the costs of losing an average performer. The true costs are hard to estimate. They include investments in the employee's development; the loss of knowledge and experience gained, and lost productivity.

The cost components of staff turnover include separations costs (associated with pay, administration, exit interview); replacement costs (advertising, interviewing, screening, administration); training costs (formal and informal); and other, intangible, costs associated with a reduction in productivity or quality, increased workloads and stress.

WHERE'S THE DATA?

Data on staff turnover can be gathered from the payroll system. Costs associated with the turnover can be calculated by estimating the individual components listed in the previous section.

CALCULATING IT — AN EXAMPLE

Let us take as an example an organization which has 500 employees at the start of the month and takes on no new recruits in that period.

During the month, the following information was recorded in the company's HR files:

Deaths	2
Accidents (employees no longer able to do the work)	2
Resignations	5
Dismissals	1

$$\text{Voluntary turnover rate} = \frac{5}{\text{Average no. of employees during the month}}$$

$$= \frac{5}{\left(\frac{500 + 490}{2}\right)} \times 100\%$$

$$= 1.01\% \text{ per month or } 12.12\% \text{ per year}$$

What it Means

There are any number of conclusions that can be drawn from the fact that an organization has a high voluntary-turnover rate. It may be, for example, that it is performing badly as a consequence of having an unhealthy organizational culture, with inadequate appraisal, recognition and reward programs or poor leadership. Or its selection processes may be in need of complete overhaul to ensure that the job and the individual chosen to do it are well matched.

25

Competency–development Expense Per Employee

THE DEFINITION

Competency-development expense (CDE) per employee is a measure of the costs incurred in developing identified competencies for each full-time equivalent (FTE) employee in any given year. These competencies identified for development are aligned with organizational strategy and directly related to helping employees achieve business objectives.

THE FORMULA

$$\text{CDE per employee} = \frac{\text{Total CDE}}{\text{Total no. of FTE employees}}$$

THE COMPONENTS

Total CDE consists of all expenses and investments made by the organization in activities and initiatives related to the development of specific competencies or capabilities required for business success.

In calculating these expenses, account should be taken of opportunity costs associated with the participant's time that could have been spent in other activities; the direct costs of training programs and associated travel and accommodation expenses; the costs incurred in developing or improving training infrastructure; and the costs associated with using outside training providers and coaches.

Total no. of FTE employees covers all full-time and full-time equivalent staff employed by the enterprise during a given period.

Year-on-year comparisons and graphs by division/department can be useful for plotting trends and highlighting variances.

WHERE'S THE DATA?

The data regarding the different components of CDE can be obtained from the organization's financial reports. The FTE figures are shown in the payroll system.

CALCULATING IT — AN EXAMPLE

XYZ Inc. runs a skills-development program, in which five of its 100 full-time employees will take part at any one time. XYZ usually runs the program three times a year.

Assume that:

- opportunity cost per employee per day = US$500 (salary + lost revenue)
- fixed cost per session of five employees = US$10,000
- investment in infrastructure = US$30,000
- HR administration cost = US$1,000

$$\text{Therefore, total CDE} = (3 \times 5 \text{ employees} \times 500)$$
$$+ (3 \times 10,000)$$
$$+ 30,000 + 1,000$$
$$= \text{US\$68,500}$$

$$\text{The CDE per employee} = \frac{\text{US\$68,500}}{100}$$
$$= \text{US\$685}$$

WHAT IT MEANS

Mapping trends over time provides a clear indication of the commitment of the organization to develop the capacity of its employees. If the CDE figure increases over time and/or is higher than the industry average, the organization is making an effort to invest time and money to develop its key capabilities.

If the ratio is falling and/or is below the industry average, there is a danger that the organization may be falling behind competitors and/or may not be developing required competencies at a sufficiently fast pace.

26 Training Hours Per Employee

THE DEFINITION

This is a measure of the average number of hours spent by an organization's employees on training activities. The need for training may arise as a result of new technology or new processes being introduced into the workplace. It also becomes necessary when employees are moved from one department to another. Employees are increasingly being given training in "soft" areas such as communication skills to improve group operations and to improve customer focus. Developing skills is a lifelong process and continues beyond the basic training given to employees when they join the organization.

THE FORMULA

$$\text{Training hours per employee} = \frac{\text{Total no. of hours of training for all employees}}{\text{No. of employees}}$$

THE COMPONENTS

The training undertaken by employees during the period under consideration can broadly be classified into two areas: in core business process and technology; and in soft skills, such as developing communication skills.

Training hours can be compared on a monthly, quarterly, semi-annual or annual basis. In knowledge-based organizations, it is common practice to include training hours in the performance-review scorecards of employees to keep track of the organization's efforts to develop employees' skills.

The number of training hours provides a good gauge of the company's overall training efforts. It is important to get training right. Inefficient training programs can result in increased costs and organizational disruption arising from a high turnover of staff, reduced efficiency, the need for greater supervision, and low motivation in the workforce.

WHERE'S THE DATA?

The data can usually be obtained from the HR or training departments.

CALCULATING IT — AN EXAMPLE

Let's take an example of a small software company with 100 employees. Assume that 25 of these take 100 hours of training in a year, 40 take 80 hours of training and the rest take 65 hours of training.

Then the average number of training hours per employee for that year would be calculated as follows:

$$\frac{[(25 \times 100) + (40 \times 80) + (35 \times 65)]}{100} = 79.75$$

WHAT IT MEANS

In our example, the company is performing below the industry average of 82 hours per employee per year. The figures show that 75% of its workforce receives training that is below the industry average. However, the average number of training hours per employee, at almost 80 hours, is near the industry's average. This organization may want to look more closely at who is the beneficiary of the training, who has missed out, and whether the training invested can be directly correlated to high levels of performance, to higher productivity or, indeed, to the opposite. This indicator can also help the organization decide where to focus its training programs in order to help create a more efficient workforce.

The number of training hours per employee is an indirect measure for assessing the value the organization places on its workers.

MAGIC NUMBER 27

Cost Per Trainee Hour

THE DEFINITION

Cost per trainee hour is a measure of the average cost per hour an organization incurs on training its employees over a given time period. This can be an indicator of how much importance an organization pays to upgrading the skills of its employees relative to other organizations in the industry.

THE FORMULA

$$\text{Cost per trainee hour} = \frac{\text{Total training cost (direct and indirect)}}{\text{Total no. of trainees} \times \text{Total no. of training hours}}$$

THE COMPONENTS

Direct costs are expenses tied specifically to providing a training course and include the wages and benefits paid to trainees and instructors for the duration of the course, the cost of providing office space and equipment, the cost of preparing instructional materials as well as travel expenses and the fees paid for external training services.

Indirect costs are expenses which are typically not charged to a training program, such as the lost production, missed sales, staff replacement costs and reduced productivity while trainees are participating in learning programs.

No. of trainees refers to those who are undergoing the training course.

No. of training hours is the number of hours spent by an employee on a training course.

WHERE'S THE DATA?

Reliable estimates of the direct costs associated with training are obtainable from the organization's payroll, budget and accounting records, or from the comptroller's office. The number of hours spent on the training will be recorded in employees' individual training schedules.

CALCULATING IT — AN EXAMPLE

Ten welders from an engineering company are to attend a two-day course on welding techniques. The training lasts for five hours each day. The company's hourly wage for welders is $15.

Total trainee cost $= 10 \times 2 \times 15 \times 5 = \$1{,}500$

The course instructor is also an employee of the company and his hourly wage is $25. In addition to the two days' training, he requires a full day's preparation time (eight hours).

The instructor's cost $= 25 \times 8 + (2 \times 25 \times 5) = \$450$
Total cost for trainees and instructor $= 1{,}500 + 450$
$$= \$1{,}950$$

The content of the course has been supplied by an external content developer, who charges $225 per day for his services. He spends four days preparing the course. He spends $250 on instructional materials.

$$\text{Total content preparation cost} = 4 \times 225 + 250$$
$$= \$1,150$$

This is a practical course and the company is obliged to spend another $200 on welding rods.

A pipe welding machine with an estimated useful life of 10 years has been purchased exclusively for training purposes, at a cost of $24,000. The machine has a yearly maintenance cost of $1,000, and it will be used for 10 courses per year.

$$\text{Annual equipment purchase cost} = \frac{24,000}{10} + 1,000$$
$$= \$3,400$$
$$\text{Total purchased equipment cost per course} = \frac{3,400}{10}$$
$$= \$340$$

In addition to all the above, there is a daily rental charge of $100 for the training room. The total rental charge is therefore $200.

$$\text{Thus, the total cost of the course} = 1,950 + 1,150 + 200 + 340 + 200$$
$$= \$3,840$$

The total training cost per employee is therefore $384 (3,840/10), making the total training cost per employee per hour $38.40 (384/10).

WHAT IT MEANS

Analyzing the cost of training per trainee hour provides useful information for planning and budgetary purposes. It can help determine the cost-effectiveness of current training delivery methods and whether the system needs to be overhauled.

28 Percentage of Employees Trained, by Category

THE DEFINITION

This measures the number of employees in a particular work category who receive training and expresses it as a percentage of the total training given across the organization. Obviously, different companies in different industries may choose to categorize their employees in different ways. For example, training may be given for specific activities (induction, preparation for accreditation or licensing, compliance, changes in work practice, technology upgrades) in accordance with different departmental needs or at different managerial levels. The nature of their individual work contracts may also determine the type and frequency of training employees receive.

This measure gives an indication of where the organization is investing, or not investing, in developing the skills of its employees. This information enables organizations to determine correlations between levels of training and optimized productivity.

THE FORMULA

Percentage of employees trained, by category

$$= \frac{\text{No. of employees in job category receiving training}}{\text{Total no. of employees trained}}$$

THE COMPONENTS

The total number of employees trained in the organization would take into account all the training programs conducted by the organization and all the employees (irrespective of the category) who were enrolled for those programs. These programs may include induction training for new employees, cross-functional training and training in new technology, among others.

Employees trained in a particular category takes into account the number of people from a particular function/department where training has been provided.

WHERE'S THE DATA?

The number of employees in the organization can be easily obtained from the payroll system. The HR department will generally keep a record of any training that takes place throughout the organization.

CALCULATING IT — AN EXAMPLE

A consumer-goods company has 220 staff across a number of departments, as follows:

Department	Number of Employees
Marketing	50
Sales	100
Finance	30
Human Resources	20
Logistics	20
Total	**220**

The number of employees given training last year are listed by department below:

Department	Number of Employees
Marketing	10
Sales	30
Finance	5
Human Resources	2
Logistics	5
Total	**52**

Applying the formula to the marketing department, for example, is straightforward:

$$\frac{\text{No. trained in marketing}}{\text{Total no. of employees trained}} = \frac{10}{52} \times 100\%$$

$$= 19.23\%$$

Similar calculations can be performed for each of the various departments.

WHAT IT MEANS

This metric gives an indication about levels of investment and the focus of training programs within the company — for example, what percentage of employees has been given induction training, and how much has been provided in the area of technology-upgrade programs. Thus the management can get to know whether the training programs are focusing on developing a particular category of employees. The figures can be compared with those of other companies in its industry to show where the organization stands in this regard.

The effectiveness of this measure can be increased by combining it with the data on the percentage of employees trained within different functions. Plotted over time, comparisons will indicate the direction and focus of the training and development programs and whether they are adapting to new circumstances.

Part Three

Magic Numbers for Talent and Reward

Magic Numbers for Talent and Reward

In this section, we will look at the metrics used to measure talent management within an organization and the methods used to measure how that talent is rewarded. These measures are set out in the following "magic numbers":

29. Internal-hire probability

30. Retention rate of key employees

31. Range (distribution) of performance-appraisal ratings

32. Job evaluation

33. Firm salary/competitor salary ratio

34. Incentive compensation differential

35. The Black-Scholes method of calculating stock-option values

36. Total compensation expense per employee

29 Internal-hire Probability

THE DEFINITION

Internal-hire probability P(IH) measures the likelihood of an existing employee being selected for a position that becomes available within the organization.

THE FORMULA

$$P(IH) = \frac{\text{Total number of positions filled from within}}{\text{Total number of positions available}} \times 100\%$$

THE COMPONENTS

The *number of positions available* refers to positions within the organization that are open either to internal applicants only, or to both internal and external applicants, within a given period.

The *number of positions filled from within* obviously refers to those which are taken up by internal appointments.

These figures can be broken down further to analyze appointments to positions across different levels of the company's hierarchy or within specific divisions and departments.

WHERE'S THE DATA?

This information is typically available in the organization's HR information system.

CALCULATING IT — AN EXAMPLE

Number of positions open to internal and external applicants across the company in the last 12 months = 50

Number of those positions filled by existing employees = 14

Therefore:

$$\text{Internal-hire probability} = \frac{14}{50} \times 100\%$$
$$= 28\%$$

WHAT IT MEANS

In situations where available jobs are open to internal applicants only, if the P(IH) is higher than the industry norm, this may indicate that the organization believes in fostering talent from within and is committed to building the careers of its employees.

An organization which has a strong focus on providing career-development paths for its employees is likely to look to internal candidates to fill any vacancies that become available.

If the P(IH) is low against industry norms, it may be that the organization is failing to capitalize on the skills and potential which exist internally. A tendency to "buy" rather than build from within may lead to dissatisfaction within the existing workforce and result in greater staff turnover.

30 Retention Rate of Key Employees

THE DEFINITION

This metric reflects the percentage of key employees retained by the organization over a given period. It is an indicator of the extent to which such individuals are engaged in and satisfied with the organization as a place to work. The degree of engagement has a direct correlation with the organization's success.

Key employees are those who show consistent high performance, exceeding expectations, over three or more consecutive performance periods. They possess skills or knowledge that is unique and/or highly valued by the organization and are currently performing well in a critical area of the organization's operations. These individuals have been identified against an agreed set of criteria as having high potential to take on key roles in the future.

THE FORMULA

Retention rate of key employees

$$= \frac{\text{No. remaining at end of time period}}{\text{Total no. identified at start of time period}} \times 100\%$$

THE COMPONENTS

For this metric to be of any value, the organization must first have a clear definition of what it means by "key employees" and a set of criteria against which this can be measured. These criteria will, of course, be determined in accordance with the organization's business strategy, culture, critical capabilities and performance-reward strategy. In addition to the qualities and characteristics outlined above, the organization will also take into consideration critical or rare skills that are not easily replaced or which prove valuable to competitors if the individual possessing those skills were to leave.

The retention rate is generally measured over a 12-month period.

Where's the Data?

The necessary information can be obtained from payroll and HR records.

Calculating it — an Example

The calculation is straightforward. Let's assume that the number of key employees identified at the start of the year is 50. Of these, 22 remain with the organization at the end of the period.

$$\text{Retention rate} = \frac{22}{50} \times 100\%$$
$$= 44\%$$

What it Means

A high retention rate compared with industry norms would tend to indicate that there is a high level of engagement and satisfaction amongst key employees. This reflects well on the organization's culture and is likely to make an attractive proposition for outside talent. If the retention rate is low against industry norms, however, the costs (in both time and money) involved in replacing key employees will be high. This will be reflected in the company's results and in its relationships with its customers. Low retention may also indicate that the organization's culture does not present the kind of opportunities for development or financial rewards that will keep key staff sufficiently interested in their work.

Range (Distribution) of Performance–appraisal Ratings

THE DEFINITION

Companies typically evaluate the performance of their employees on a half-yearly or annual basis. These performance ratings are based on a set of predetermined objectives or goals set and agreed upon by the supervisor and the employee. These goals are tied to the business goals of the organization. The ratings form the basis for annual compensation and promotions.

The variable pay distribution by performance ratings, as illustrated in Figure 3, shows the relationship between the performance rating an individual receives as a result of his/her performance over a given review period, and the incentive or bonus amount (s)he is awarded.

By plotting these data and constructing a line of best fit, it is possible to assess the strength of the relationship. If the organization has a strong pay-for-performance culture, skills and the right tools and processes, it would be expected that the relationship would be strong and positive. That is, the higher the performance rating, the greater the incentive amount.

THE FORMULA

Performance ratings are typically made across performance categories, ranging from very low (fails to meet targets/expectations) through to very high (significantly exceeds targets/expectations).

Ratings may be in *absolute* terms (that is, as determined by the employee's manager alone), or in *relative* terms. Relative performance

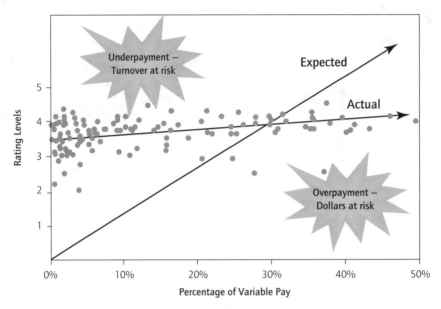

Figure 3   Variable pay distribution by performance ratings

assessment (RPA) is a concept in which managers' assessments of the performance of their staff is compared and ratings are awarded relatively.

For example, managers meet to compare the relative performance of staff under their supervision. Depending on the type of RPA used by the organization, they are asked to categorize or "fit" the performance of each person under a curve. Typical ranking distributions methods are:

Ranking Type	How it works
Bell Curve	1. 10% are top performers, exceeding expectations 2. 80% are the backbone, meeting expectations 3. 10% are not meeting expectations
Stacking	One individual is at the very top, someone else is at the very bottom and everyone else is ranked consecutively in between, based on performance
Quartiles	Employees are ranked and divided into quartiles

Managers are advised on how to align ranking allocations across similar roles, so that the overall organizational distribution is achieved.

THE COMPONENTS

- Absolute and/or relative performance rating score or category for a given performance review period. This can be, for example, on a scale of 1 (far below expectations) to 5 (far exceeded expectations).

- Percentage of variable pay, expressed as a percentage of base salary.

WHERE'S THE DATA?

Performance-appraisal data can be typically found in an organization's HR information system. Some organizations record and store such data using Performance Management System (PMS) software.

Similarly, the percentage of variable pay awarded often resides in the compensation module of an organization's HR information system, in a separate spreadsheet, or is tracked by HR.

CALCULATING IT — AN EXAMPLE

Using data from the previous appraisal period, plot each employee's performance rating against variable incentive pay (see "Actual" curve in Figure 3) received.

Using statistical software, conduct a regression analysis on the data to identify the line of best fit.

WHAT IT MEANS

The results can be used to determine if the organization is truly paying for performance, overpaying for underperformance or underpaying for high performance.

How is this done? The resulting graph shows the difference between the actual relationship and the expected relationship the organization hopes to achieve between pay and performance.

If the actual line of best fit is flat (that is, there is little or no relationship), there is little differentiation between the incentives for poor, average or high performers. This indicates that there is a real risk that the organization is overpaying average and lower performers — that is, it is "throwing money away" for very little return, if any, for its investment. There is also a real risk that the organization will lose those higher performers, who are likely to be disgruntled with their perceived underpayment for the level of performance they delivered.

Under such circumstances, the organization probably does not have the right systems in place to drive a performance culture and differentiate performance with differentiated pay. Not only has the incentive' pool been inefficiently utilized, but the organization might soon lose its top performers to competitors who truly do pay for performance.

Finally, the distribution of points along the graph also hints at where the performance ratings of the organization's employees are clustered. If predominantly clustered in the middle (for example, at "3"), too high or too low, there is an indication that managers are not differentiating performance sufficiently. This may be due to a lack of skill and/or confidence in setting targets and in evaluating performance and/or the courage to give true performance feedback.

Job Evaluation

THE DEFINITION

Job evaluation is a method of assessing the work value of positions within an organization. It provides a systematic, defensible approach for grading positions within a job-classification system. Thus, it provides a sound basis for pay decisions and HR management. Job evaluation also fits into a broad network of HR management activities.

THE FORMULA

Job evaluation is usually undertaken using three different but complementary techniques to make judgments about the relative worth of a job: whole-of-job benchmarking; comparison to narrative standards; and points-factor evaluation. Each has its merits and disadvantages, but the points-factor evaluation is a quantifiable tool that is generally accepted.

There are many points-factor evaluation systems in use around the world that have been created by companies to suit their own requirements or by consulting firms that offer tools that can be applied across an organization's global operations. The factors reflect the dimensions of work that are regarded as the key determinants of work value.

The one illustrated here is the International Position-Evaluation system (IPE), which was created decades ago and has been reformed many times to keep it clear, consistent and simple to apply. As summarized in Figure 4 below, it measures work in terms of four major factors and 10 dimensions. Essentially job evaluators make judgments against defined standards for each of the 10 dimensions — in total, there are

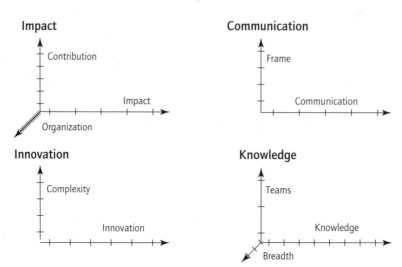

Figure 4   The international position-evaluation system

63 points on the scale. At the end of the process, the work value of a job is determined in terms of a numeric position class (PC).

THE COMPONENTS

The job-evaluation system is designed to measure the relative size of positions. Information used in the job-evaluation process may come from specifically designed questionnaires completed by position holders, from interviews with position holders or managers, and/or from position descriptions.

In conducting evaluations, a position is measured in terms of the actual requirements of the position, rather than the experience or skills possessed by the particular person in the job.

In job evaluation, each position's requirements are compared with detailed standard definitions to find the level of each sub-factor which most accurately describes the characteristics of the position. Once each sub-factor has been assessed, work-value points can be determined. Mathematically derived point grids are used to assign numerical values (points) to factors. The total of the points assigned for all factors is the work-value score for the position and represents the relative size of the position.

Common-sense judgments apply in this system. In most cases, it will be self-evident which level applies to a particular position and difficulties will normally arise only where incomplete or insufficient information is available. Nonetheless, the process of job evaluation is a skill which is acquired through training and experience.

Before starting the evaluation process you will need to have had specific training and supervised experience. There are few benefits to be gained from reading the manual on its own. You must have comprehensive information about and understanding of each position and the environment in which it operates. This is gained from a questionnaire, interview, position description, field visit and/or by talking to people who understand the job well. In this last regard, it is important to use the judgments of at least two other people, including someone from the organization who is familiar with the position under review. You must have specific information to assess the impact/value of a specific dimension of the job (for example, expenditure, revenue, scope of projects, nature of the service, etc). Needless to say, you should record the outcome of each evaluation.

In undertaking any job evaluation you must keep in mind that it is the position that is being evaluated, not the position holder. Bear in mind, too, that an evaluation measures position content, not the position title. Supply-and-demand factors may affect a person's pay but do not influence the evaluation of a position. It is important to remember that this process is a systematic, rather than a scientific, way of making sound judgments.

WHERE'S THE DATA?

The process of points-factor evaluation creates a ranking of jobs with the individual ratings that have led to that score. This in turn can be translated into organization charts that illustrate the differences across jobs in the organizational context, as shown in Figures 5 and 6 below.

WMM PC	Actual Position Title	Size	Impact			Communication				Innovation				Knowledge			
			Impact Degree	Contribution Degree	Points	Communication Degree	Frame Degree	Points		Innovation Degree	Complexity Degree	Points	Knowledge Degree	Team Degree	Breadth Degree	Points	
61	General Manager	2	4	5	167	5	4	115		4	4	80	6	3	1	195
49	Information Service	2	2.5	3	80	3	1	40		3.5	3	63	4	1	1	90
55	Registration Manager	2	3.5	4	135	4	4	100		3	3	50	5	1.5	1	131
56	Admin Manager	2	3.5	4	135	3.5	3	70		3.5	3	63	5	3	1	173
58	Marketing Manager	2	3.5	5	149	4	4	100		4	3	75	4.5	3	1	162
53	Product Manager	2	3	3	97	3	3	60		4	2	70	4	2	1	125
53	Sales Manager	2	3	3	97	4	4	100		3	3	50	4	2	1	125
49	BKK/UPC Rep	2	2	3	63	3	4	75		3	3	50	3.5	1	1	75
50	Clinical Research Assistant	2	2.5	3	80	3	2	55		3.5	3	63	4	1	1	90
52	Logistic Manager	2	3	3	97	3.5	4	88		3.5	3	63	4	1	1	90
56	Medical Manager	2	4	3	144	3.5	2	65		4	3	75	5	2	1	148
60	Deputy General Manager	2	4	4	153	4.5	4	108		4	4	80	6	3	1	195
57	National Sales Manager	2	3.5	4	135	4	4	100		4	3	75	4.5	3	1	162
55	Institutional Business Manager	2	3.5	4	135	4	4	100		3.5	3	63	4.5	1.5	1	162
53	Product Manager	2	3	3	97	4	4	100		4	3	75	4	1	1	90

Figure 5   Putting value on a job position

Before and After Job Evaluation

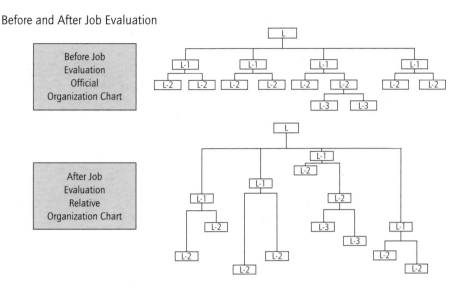

Figure 6   The result of proper job evaluation

The final step in the process is to create a job-grading structure that groups jobs into bands or levels with similar characteristics, as illustrated in Figure 7.

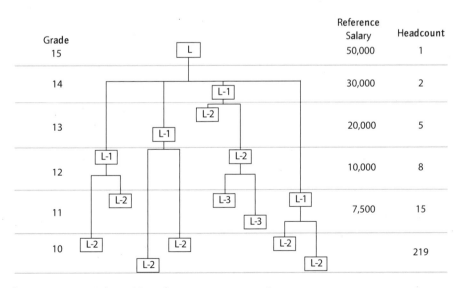

Figure 7   Using job positions for proper remuneration

WHAT IT MEANS

A job-grade or classification structure can provide a number of significant benefits for an organization. In simple terms, it provides a convenient means of:

- grouping jobs of similar work value into a sensible hierarchy of responsibilities

- identifying the career structure available within an organization

- identifying the common set of work-level standards and competencies required for particular groups of jobs

- indicating rank or status within an organization

- developing a framework for pay ranges and benefits programs.

In the same way that the point score from the job-evaluation system identifies the relative work value between jobs, a job-grading system identifies the relativities between "clusters" or groups of jobs and also provides for simpler administration of a range of other matters. The major benefits of a points-factor job-evaluation system in this situation lie in the definition of the job grades and the ongoing classification of jobs into grades.

33 Firm Salary/Competitor Salary Ratio

THE DEFINITION

Firm salary/competitor salary ratio is the ratio of the salary the firm is offering to its employees compared to the salary its competitors are offering to their employees for a similar kind of job profile. This ratio is the indicator of the firm's potential and capability to attract and retain the right quality of people it needs vis-à-vis its competitors.

THE FORMULA

$$\text{Firm salary/competitor salary ratio} = \frac{\text{Salary paid by the company}}{\text{Average salary paid by competitors}}$$

For different posts and job profiles there will be different set of ratios. This evaluation can be done on a monthly or annual basis.

THE COMPONENTS

Firm salary is the sum of basic salary allowances and other benefits including insurance, children's education loan, conveyance allowance, housing allowance, bonus, incentives, ESOPS (Employee Share Option Schemes), health coverage, increment, among others, paid to the employee for a particular period, either on a monthly or yearly basis.

Similarly, *competitor salary* is the salary offered by a competitor to its employees (the basic composition remaining the same as above) for the same kind of responsibilities performed for the corresponding period.

This ratio helps in restructuring the pay process so that the firm can remain competitive in attracting and retaining the right talent from the job market.

However, there are other factors which can influence a potential employee's choice of employer. These might include:

- brand name — some employees prefer to work in a well-known/ famous firm because of its brand name and reputation, even if this firm's salary is not as competitive as that of its competitors.

- size of the firm — the size of the employer's firm/operations can be an important consideration for some potential employees. Some prospective employees look towards a large firm as an open field, offering immense opportunities and learning experience, which a smaller firm may not be able to give.

- work environment — a healthy working environment and a collegial work culture is what many employees prefer over higher remuneration.

- incentives composition — for some employees, the composition of incentives (monetary and non-monetary) can be an important criterion when it comes to selecting an employer. Firms that offer better performance-based incentives may be preferred to higher-salary-paying competitors.

WHERE'S THE DATA?

The sources of this information are varied and include compensation consultants who conduct benchmark salary surveys that use standard definitions of compensation to allow for cross-company/cross-industry comparisons. In many countries, the labor department, too, conducts periodic surveys in major metropolitan labor markets. Employers' and other professional associations are other potential sources of data. In some cases, because of the issue of data compatibility, some HR departments conduct their own salary surveys.

CALCULATING IT — AN EXAMPLE

We can calculate the firm salary/competitor salary ratios for different employers and see the effect of the ratios on their competitiveness for attracting and retaining the best talent.

Employer	Salary paid by firm	Average salary paid by competitors	Firm salary/competitor salary ratio
Employer 1	$9,800	$10,000	.98
Employer 2	$15,000	$15,000	1.00
Employer 3	$20,000	$23,000	.87
Employer 4	$20,000	$32,000	.63

In the above table, we get different firm salary/competitor salary ratios under different salary cases, each of which has different implications for the competitive standing of the firm as far as hiring and retaining the best talent is concerned. For example, Employer 2 has the most competitive ratio of 1.00 (15,000/15,000). At this ratio, Employer 2 is providing salaries that are on a par with the industry average. Employer 4, on the other hand, has the worst ratio, .63, which makes him the least competitive in hiring and retaining the most talented employees.

WHAT IT MEANS

Trends over time will provide a clear indication that if the ratio is greater than 1 there is a greater likelihood that, from the point of view of compensation, the company will be able to attract new employees and retain its current staff (assuming other factors remain constant).

If the ratio shows a downward trend, however, this is a matter of concern and the company may need to revise its salary structure if the ratio is considerably below 1 and staff turnover is an issue.

Comparisons of firm/competitor salary ratio by job function provide an idea of what functions competitors are giving more importance.

34 Incentive Compensation Differential

THE DEFINITION

Compensation refers to all forms of financial returns and tangible services and benefits employees receive as part of an employment relationship.

Total compensation includes pay received directly as cash (for example, base wages, merit increases, incentives, and cost-of-living adjustments) or indirectly through benefits and services (for example, pensions, health insurance, paid time off).

An incentive is a reward for a specific behavior, designed to encourage a certain set of behaviors. When we talk about "incentive compensation", we are referring to the rewards given in terms of cash or indirect benefits and services for a specific behavior. Most incentive programs are either cash or equity based.

THE FORMULA

For the purposes of illustration, we define incentive differential in monetary terms only. The non-monetary benefits are ignored as they are more or less subjective in nature and cannot be quantified. To make it simple, we shall ignore equity-based reward as well.

$$\text{Incentive compensation differential} = \frac{\begin{array}{c}\text{Monetary incentives to}\\\text{high performers} -\\\text{monetary incentives}\\\text{to low performers}\end{array}}{\begin{array}{c}\text{Monetary incentives}\\\text{to high performers}\end{array}} \times 100\%$$

THE COMPONENTS

The *incentive compensation differential* is the percentage difference in the compensation of gross benefits and services given to high and low performers with the same job profile within an organization.

An incentive plan has both monetary and non-monetary elements.

The *monetary* benefits may be in the form of cash (for example, cash-based bonuses, stocks, and stock options) or in kind (for example, movie tickets, coupons redeemable at stores, membership of clubs, paid time off, training, gifts, free lunches and picnics).

The benefits in kind have an opportunity cost and hence could be translated to monetary benefit. The opportunity cost is the total cost of obtaining the benefits in kind (for example, training) that, if not awarded, would require the individual employees to pay for out of their own pocket.

There is a *non-monetary* component related to the moral incentives which an employee expects for a good performance. If she behaves as expected, she may expect the approval or even the admiration of other members of her working group or organization and enjoy an enhanced sense of acceptance or self-esteem, as reflected in the form of letters of appreciation/or recognition, dinners with the boss, special assignments and trophies. But it is difficult to quantify these awards in monetary terms.

Since desired personal outcomes (promotions, raises) are usually preceded by social approval, people will engage in behaviors that receive social recognition and avoid behaviors that lead to the disapproval of others.

Providing a clear definition of "performance" is probably the most important step in establishing any incentive plan. It tells the employee what output or behavior the organization considers important enough to reward — that is, to spend its money on. Such a definition should be complete, or the organization will not obtain the outcomes it needs from its employees.

The most common definition of performance, and in many ways the best, is the intended output of the job. In some situations this can be made an explicitly measurable item, such as the number of electronic assemblies produced. The most common incentive plan that uses an output measure is piecework. In this plan, a set reward value is attached to each unit of output; the employee's pay is that value multiplied by the number of units produced.

An alternative measure is time required to complete a task. Amount of production and amount of time are two variables that are always considered together in individual incentive plans. The most common form of a time-rate individual incentive is the standard-hour plan. As in piecework, the employee is paid according to output.

Under another plan, formal production standards are determined for the job, and the employee's performance is judged against those standards. Evaluation is done at least quarterly and the pay rate may be adjusted according to how well the employee has performed in comparison with the standards.

A single dimension, such as units produced in a piecework plan, is appealing for its simplicity and clear performance–reward connections but is often dysfunctional when it comes to genuine productivity. The clearest example of this is the problem of quality in a piecework plan. If the number of units is the only performance standard, the employee is encouraged to turn out as many units as possible, but the units will likely be substandard. Many incentive plans therefore employ multiple performance definitions and the question becomes how to combine them. The simplest way, if possible, is to use a composite score, in which the values of various performance variables are added together.

WHERE'S THE DATA?

The performance that is evaluated may take the form of either outcomes of the work or the activity and behavior involved in it. Performance appraisal works by comparing an employee's contribution with some standard. The standard may be a set of criteria or some other employee(s). It is the performance standard that defines what the organization considers to be performance. The job description should be the place to find the important performance standards for the job.

Monetary benefits: The high and low performers can be identified from their performance appraisals. The monetary benefits which the company gives for their performance are available from the payroll system.

Non-monetary benefits: The formal non-monetary benefits, such as awards and decorations, are available in the company records. Information on the informal non-monetary benefits, such as dinner with the boss, is completely unavailable.

CALCULATING IT — AN EXAMPLE

Position: Plant Manager

Assume that his performance is evaluated across technical skills, quality of work, interpersonal skills, communication skills, approach to work, quantity of work, supervisory skills and leadership skills. Let the maximum points that can be attained by an individual be 100.

Let the monthly base pay be $10,000.

Assumptions:

- Maximum medical benefits payable for a year is $60,000
- Maximum profit sharing for a particular year for an employee is $60,000
- Maximum value of goods for which discount is given in a year is $25,000

- Maximum transportation payable for a year is $25,000

- Education expenditure refers to the training programs sponsored by the company for its employees.

Let's say that in the current year the high-performing employee receives a cumulative score of 95 in his appraisal. Based on a preset table of what he would be awarded, his incentive compensation works out to $209,820.

On the other hand, a low-performing employee gets a score of 17. His incentive compensation is $31,581.

$$\text{Incentive compensation differential} = \frac{209,820 - 31,581}{209,820} \times 100\%$$

$$= 85\%$$

WHAT IT MEANS

A high incentive compensation differential infuses a competitive spirit within the company as everyone would aim towards performing above the standards to obtain maximum benefits, which would inevitably lead the organization towards better performance.

The huge incentive compensation differential evident in our example implies that the company believes that the monetary benefit is the most important motivator for an individual. While this may be true, the company must reinforce these monetary benefits with the non-monetary rewards to obtain the full benefit.

The huge differential also helps the company in cutting the cost of labor to a great extent as it ensures that individuals are rewarded according to their respective contributions to the company.

If the incentive compensation differential is very low in comparison to what can be attained — say, in our example the attained differential is only 20% — then all the following issues need to be clarified:

- the performance standards may be very high

- the performance standards are not being communicated properly.

- the monetary benefits may not have been reinforced with non-monetary benefits

- the performance appraisal may not be able to capture all the aspects of performance properly and may have to be redesigned

- the performance evaluators may need to undergo training

- the employees may lack the required skills to perform their tasks properly.

The Black–Scholes Method of Calculating Stock-option Values

THE DEFINITION

The Black-Scholes model was published by Fisher Black and Myron Scholes, two finance professors, in 1973.[1] It is of great importance in modern finance and has become one of the most popular option-pricing models. It is noted for its relative simplicity, with an analytical, closed-end solution, its efficiency of computation — up to 100 times faster than an alternative binomial stock-option pricing model — and its assumption of normal distribution of returns on assets, which is widely accepted to be a reasonable premise.

A stock option (more precisely, a "call" option) is the right (but not the obligation) to buy a share of stock for a predetermined price sometime during a given period of time, regardless of the actual market value. An example of this would be the right to buy a share of stock in IBM for $100 at any time in the next 10 years.

Employee stock options (ESOs) are used by companies to reward and retain key employees. A distinct feature of ESOs is that an employee who has been granted an option must wait until the option vests (that is, until such time it can be traded) before the option may be converted into shares of company stock. ESOs vest in accord with the employee stock-option plan (ESOP). If the employee leaves the company, he normally loses options that have not yet vested.

The Black-Scholes model is one of two approaches used by most companies today to value their ESOs. It has five key determinants of a call option's price:

- stock price, prevailing price

- strike price/exercise price

- volatility of the stock

- time to expiry

- risk-free interest rate.

THE FORMULA

The original formula for calculating the theoretical option price (OP) is as follows:

$$OP = SN(d_1) - Xe^{-it} N(d_2)$$

Where:

$$d_1 = \frac{\ln\left(\frac{S}{X}\right) + \left(r + \frac{v^2}{2}\right) t}{v\sqrt{t}}$$
$$d_2 = d_1 - v\sqrt{t}$$

The Components

S $=$ stock price
X $=$ strike price/exercise price
t $=$ time remaining until expiry, expressed as a percent of a year
r $=$ current continuously compounded risk-free interest rate
v $=$ annual volatility of stock price (the standard deviation of the shareholder returns over one year)
ln $=$ natural logarithm
$N(x)$ $=$ standard normal cumulative distribution function
e $=$ the exponential function

The Black-Scholes method is for a call that can be exercised only at the maturity date — what is known as a "European call". Some options give the buyer or holder an additional right to exercise not only at the maturity date but also on any date before then. These are known as "American options".

Since an American option gives an extra right, it must be worth at least as much as a European option and could be worth more. An ESOP has some of the flexibility features of American options as it can be exercised before the maturity date but after the vesting period.

WHERE'S THE DATA?

The stock price and risk-free interest rate can be obtained from public sources such as Research Insight and Datastream. The option term and strike price information are available from the company concerned. The annual volatility has to be calculated using the stock price information.

CALCULATING IT — AN EXAMPLE

Suppose a company wants to give its employees stock options. The company's stock currently trades at US$50 and the option's strike price is US$55. The option will expire in three months. The stock's annual volatility is 25%. The risk-free rate is 7% per annum. What will be the price/value of the option?

Applying these values to the formula, here

$$S = 50; \ X = 55, \ v = 25\%; \ t = \frac{3}{12}; \ r = 0.07$$

$$d_1 = \frac{\ln\left(\frac{50}{55}\right) + \left\{\frac{0.07 + (0.25)^2}{2}\right\} \times 0.25}{0.25\sqrt{0.25}}$$

$d_1 = -0.5599 = -0.56 \text{ (approx)}$

$d_2 = d_1 - v\sqrt{t}$

$\quad = -0.56 - 0.25\sqrt{0.25}$

$\quad = -0.56 - 0.125 = -0.685 = -0.69 \text{ (approx)}$

$$N(d_1) = 0.2877$$
$$N(d_2) = 0.2451$$
$$\text{OP} = SN(d_1) - Xe^{-r(t)}N(d_2)$$
$$= 50 \times 0.2877 - 55 \times e^{-0.07 \times 0.25} \times 0.2451$$
$$= 14.39 - 13.25$$
$$= 1.14$$

Thus, the call option price is US$1.14.[2]

WHAT IT MEANS

Trends over time provide a clear indication that if the company performs, its stock price will rise in the long run. When the stock price rises above the strike price of ESOs, the value of ESOs will increase and, more importantly, the intrinsic value of ESOs (the difference between the market price and strike price) will increase. The higher the company stock price relative to the strike price, the higher the intrinsic value of ESOs. Consequently, employees holding ESOs will see their wealth growing when the company performs.

If the company underperforms, its stock price will decrease in the long run. As the stock price drops below the strike price of ESOs, employees see the value of their holdings decrease. When the stock price is well below the strike price, the ESOs are known as "underwater ESOs" and can become worthless. This is illustrated by the experience of many US executives whose wealth, accumulated through various stock incentive programs in the 1990s, has quickly evaporated in the past few years.

It is clear that the fortunes of shareholders and employees holding ESOs are linked directly, and that the value of employee compensation moves with the market price, resulting in positive incentives.

However, the company performance can be influenced by random external factors over which employees have little control. The stock price can move up or down regardless of the performance of employees and the strategic decisions made by executives. Such movements are sometimes the result of market dynamics such as industry trends and interest-rate policies. That part of stock-price fluctuations imposes risks on employees who receive stock-option grants, resulting in negative incentives.

A careful assessment of the sources of stock-price fluctuations (or risk) has to be conducted to help calibrate the delicate balance between risk and incentives in stock-option plans.

Thus, if granted appropriately, ESOs can become an effective mechanism to motivate employees to make contributions that create value for shareholders.

The Black-Scholes model is frequently used to value the ESO grants of a company and benchmark them against its peers in defining the company's compensation strategy and stock-option plan design.

[1]   Black, F. and Scholes, M. (1973), "The pricing of options and corporate liabilities", *Journal of Political Economy*, pp. 81, 637–59.

[2]   Some stocks pay dividends. An adjustment can be made to account for the dividend effects. As the stock-option holder does not have the right to receive dividends, the dividend adjustment generally reduces the value (price) of options.

36 Total Compensation Expense Per Employee

THE DEFINITION

The provision of compensation is a systematic approach to giving monetary value to employees in exchange for work performed. Compensation may achieve several objectives, including high job satisfaction, exemplary performance and assistance in the recruitment process, all of which contribute towards furthering the company's existence. It may be adjusted in accordance with the specific requirements and purpose of the business and the resources available.

Compensation may be used to:

- recruit and retain competent employees

- boost or maintain morale/satisfaction

- reward and promote peak performance

- attain internal and external equity

- decrease staff turnover and encourage loyalty.

For many employers, recruiting and retaining the best employees is a common objective. However, the availability and salary structures of qualified employees might depend on market factors that are beyond the employer's control.

There needs to be a certain equity between the compensation which the employer is willing to pay and the sense of self-worth felt by the employee. It may be that during economic downturns, a salary freeze may result in low levels of satisfaction. On the other hand, an increase in salary levels can help reduce staff turnover. Rewards in the form of bonuses, profit sharing and stock options can also be used to encourage commendable performances.

THE FORMULA

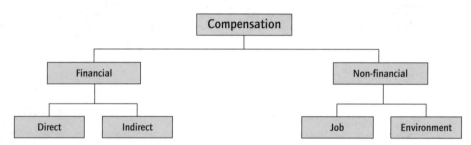

Compensation can be divided into financial compensation and non-financial compensation. Financial compensation can be further classified as direct and indirect. Direct pay would include such things as wages, salaries, commissions, overtime pay, bonuses, profit sharing, merit pay and stock options. The indirect component would include all fringe benefits such as insurance plans, social assistance, health insurance, educational assistance, paid absences, retirement benefits, and travel/meal/housing allowances.

The non-financial aspect can be broken down into the job and the work environment. The job would include interesting duties, challenges, responsibility, opportunity for recognition, the feeling of advancement and the opportunity to achieve. Environmental factors would cover factors such as sound policies, competent supervision, congenial working conditions, appropriate status symbols, flexi-time and the option of job sharing, for example.

As the non-financial aspects of compensation are not quantifiable, we shall concentrate solely on the financial component of the total compensation described above.

Based on the above, we arrive at a formula for total compensation expense per employee (TCPE) as follows:

Compensation per employee = Direct + Indirect financial benefits paid to entire full-time equivalent workforce calculated on basis of each full-time equivalent employee

$$= \frac{[(\text{Basic salary/wages} + \text{Bonus}) + (\text{Other benefits})]}{\text{Total labor force}}$$

THE COMPONENTS

The components have been described above. In this section, we will throw further light on the major sub-components that make up the overall measure.

Direct Benefits

- Salary and wages: Usually the single largest component of a compensation package, salary and wages are often the determining factor for a potential employee who is comparing competing job options. Different countries have different practices related to what constitutes salary or wages, and this can include allowances and rentals, among other things.

- Bonuses, merit pay and profit-sharing plans: These are generally paid as a lump sum at the end of a certain period and are used as a way of rewarding the employee's performance. Profit sharing is a more formal tool to reward performance but often fails to segregate individual performance from group or team performance.

- Stock options: These serve as long-term incentives and often reward employees for loyalty. They also serve as a retention tool.

Indirect Benefits

Indirect benefits are those that accrue for the employee over time and are often non-cash components of the compensation package for the employee. Major indirect benefits include health and life insurance, retirement and pension plans, paid leave, and assistance with education expenses.

Total labor force is the number of full-time equivalent staff employed by the company over the pay period under consideration, which can be weekly, fortnightly or monthly or can be grouped together to reflect a much longer time horizon.

WHERE'S THE DATA?

The data for calculating the total compensation expense per employee is obtained from the HR database and the company's payroll system.

CALCULATING IT — AN EXAMPLE

XL Technologies employs 5,000 employees on a full-time/part-time basis. The company's HR executive is looking at how to derive a figure for total compensation expense/employee to help him analyse how resources have been allocated among the employees across jobs and departments. He has at his disposal a worksheet that contains the total expenditure of the company on various items classified as direct or indirect compensation. These figures, as shown in Figure 8, are for the month of December 2004. To calculate TCPE, here's how he should proceed:

Period	From	1/12/2004
	To	31/12/2004

Expense Item	Amount ($ Million)
Wages	5.00
Commissions	1.00
Bonus	1.00
Performance Incentive	0.50
Profit Share	1.50
Allowances	2.50
Direct Benefits	**11.50**
Retirement Benefits	1.50
Health Insurance premiums	0.20
Life Insurance premiums	0.30
Paid Leave	0.50
Indirect Benefits	**2.50**
Total Compensation Expense	**14.00**

Figure 8   XL Technologies: Compensation Summary

Once the total compensation expense has been calculated as a sum of the direct and indirect benefits, the next step is to calculate the compensation cost per full-time equivalent labor force. This is necessary as some of the employees work on a part-time basis and simply relying on the total number of employees would be incorrect.

This calculation is shown in Figure 9.

No. of employees	5,000
Total full-time hours worked	720,000
Total part-time hours worked	240,000
Total no. of hours worked	960,000
Full-time hours available/month/per employee	240
Full-time equivalent labor force	**4,000**

Figure 9   Calculation of full-time equivalent labor force

The full-time equivalent workforce is derived from dividing the total number of hours worked by the number of full-time hours available per month per employee.

The next step is to calculate total compensation expense per employee. This is done by dividing total compensation expense by the full-time equivalent labor force to obtain the TCPE, as illustrated in Figure 10.

Total Compensation Expense	$14 million
Full-time equivalent labor force	4,000
Total compensation expense/employee	**$3,500**

Figure 10   Calculation of total compensation/employee

Some of the key purposes for calculating TCPE include:

- to establish a general company policy with regard to wages

- to benchmark against industry norms and prevailing market wage levels

- to calculate cost while developing financial statements/business plan

- to calculate the profit generated per employee

- to analyze indicators such as retention rate and attrition rate or turnover ratios

- as a goal-setting tool used for performance management

- to spearhead cost-cutting initiatives

- to help frame growth objectives for the company.

WHAT IT MEANS

Having a TCPE that is higher than industry norms indicates that the company's costs are higher than those of the competition. If these are higher than the limits the company has set for itself, there is clearly a need to cut costs to avoid an impending business problem. A high TCPE would reduce the profit-per-employee figures and thus affect the overall profit and profit-share per employee. To counteract this, it might well be necessary to instigate some cost-cutting measures or introduce improvements in the utilization of labor.

A low TCPE may well go hand in hand with a high attrition rate or a low retention rate.

Conclusion

In Part One, we argued that an organization can measure its workforce and HR performance *quantitatively*, in the same way it measures its other assets such as real estate, equipment, patents, brands, among others. Over time, we have witnessed a proliferation of HR measures such as payroll cost and voluntary staff-turnover rates. Most of these common HR measures focus management attention on costs and administrative needs such as recruiting.

What has been largely missing from most HR measurement practice, however, is finding the processes through which these measures can be put to strategic use. Consider this: when asked how much return they are getting on various investments associated with their workforce — such as training, incentive programs, part-time staffing, and other individual human resource practices — only a few organizations in the US knew the answer.[1] (The answer is, about 36% of an American company's revenue each year.) This is unhealthy and shows that organizations typically have the least knowledge about the return on their single largest investment — their people. Organizations often over-spend in some places and underspend in others. The good news is that, as a consequence, most companies have great potential to increase their workforce and HR performance and, subsequently, their business performance. If companies could know for certain the effects of individual HR practices, then they could configure such practices to execute their strategy more effectively.

In the main content of this book, we first catalogued the commonly used HR measures. In this concluding section, we would like to draw some salient lessons from the practice of HR measurement to truly make magic with HR numbers. They highlight challenges most organizations face in measuring their workforce and HR performance.

SYSTEMS THINKING

One salient lesson we learned from working with our clients is the need to take a new perspective on the thinking behind systems. Essentially, systems thinking helps organizations to take a fresh look at their workforce and HR performance. It also encompasses new ways of identifying and measuring workforce and HR performance, and new ways of managing people.

In essence, the development of systems thinking creates awareness of the connections that link organizational units, market dynamics, employees, processes and behaviors. Organizations are complex systems, with many linked elements and sub-systems — of which human-capital practices are just one. Organizations are, in turn, a part of a larger system which includes, among others, customers, suppliers, shareholders and the general market. A change in any part of the organization produces profound effects in others linked to this system.

The **first implication** to be drawn from this is that individual HR practices operate with varying degrees of interdependence. To understand a particular measurement fully requires that we understand how this measurement relates to and is dependent on the system. The effectiveness of one HR practice is a consequence of how that practice is aligned with the broader context of the system. For example, a compensation program that rewards individual accomplishments cannot be effective when tight collaboration needs to be in place and teamwork is the norm.

The **second implication** is that HR programs and practices that are implemented in combination can produce very different results from those that would have arisen if they had been implemented separately. For example, research in both organizational psychology and economics shows that the positive effects of organization-wide incentive plans are heightened when organizations encourage the sharing of information, employees participate in decision-making processes and when jobs are designed broadly rather than narrowly. Evidence also shows that training has its greatest impact when combined with sophisticated recruitment and selection procedures. Terms such as "interaction effect" and "complementarity" have been often used in describing this combination effect. Identification and measurement of the complementarities of HR practices can be a path to definite success.

The **third implication** is that the practice of benchmarking and, by extension, "best practices" can be fatal for making strategic workforce decisions. Any workforce and the ensuing HR measurement of it are inherently specific and unique to the organization's own environment. Benchmarking, used in isolation, pushes a company to manage its workforce according to how other companies manage them. As a result, it may focus managers on the HR measures which have little or no relation to the strategic imperatives of the firm. When that happens, the company will miss the opportunity to find the combination of HR practices that are uniquely tailored to its specific market dynamics, business model, leadership and culture. Companies with the right perspective understand that the effectiveness of HR measurement is largely dependent on the measures used being specific to the needs and practices of the organization.

DEMAND FOR THE RIGHT MEASURES

Another salient lesson for organizations seeking to make proper use of HR measurement is to make sure they "demand" the right measures. Measures matter only when they can provide guidance to decision-making and form an effective basis for performance management. Companies have had many workforce and HR measures at their disposal for years. But what measures are critical and key to the workforce decisions and, hence, the execution of business strategy? What criteria should companies use to distil those measures into a few key metrics that can focus management on key workforce factors?

The importance of an HR measure must be determined by two major factors. The first of these is the existence of a direct cause-and-effect relationship between HR measures and business outcomes. Take, for example, a statement such as the following: "Increasing the average years of service of customer-service employees by just one year would lead to a 4% increase in revenue per customer, or a total of $15 million per year." Identifying a causal relationship is always a challenge and is seldom assured solely by means of statistical modeling. At a minimum, three conditions have been identified as determinants of a cause-and-effect relationship between two variables. The first is simple correlation. The variables must move together. For example, an increase in incentive payouts is associated with an increase in labor productivity. Second, changes in the presumed causal factor must precede changes in the outcome variable; otherwise it is possible that the chain of causation can actually have occurred in reverse. For instance, companies with higher labor productivity tend to have higher profits at their disposal for higher incentive payouts. Thus, increased productivity may result in higher incentive payouts. Third, the impact of other factors that affect the outcome must be accounted for. For example, it is well known that training can lead to higher productivity. Therefore, an observed increase in labor productivity could well be the result of an increase in training, rather than an increase in incentive pay.

The second major factor is the magnitude of the impact of changes in the value of an HR measure on the value of the business outcome. Knowing the directional impact of an HR measure is not enough. The magnitude must be empirically quantified to help organizations choose from many alternative HR measures. Magnitude matters even more when executives are faced with expensive decisions about HR practices and when HR decisions involve millions of dollars.

One example of the application of this approach can be seen in the recent experience of a regional bank in the US. This bank has long known that premier customer service is what delivers improved results and has invested a great deal of time and money on research to understand its customers. Internally, it has always monitored and tracked the changes in its employees' perceptions of the company. The bank uses HR measures derived from employee-survey results to guide its employee-centered culture. Most firms would have stopped there. But the bank recognized that it was sitting on a goldmine of employee data — a running record of the workforce and performance. It took the next important step by analyzing the data, using a model and a set of statistical techniques that can discern how human-resource practices — both individually and collectively — affect important workforce and business outcomes. The study pulled together five years of data on employees and multiple years of employee surveys; data from marketing and customer research including such measures as market share, customer value and loyalty; and profitability data. The study demonstrated that, collectively, HR factors such as experience and managerial spans of control accounted for a very large proportion of the variation in the performance across regions, depending on the particular performance measures used. More importantly, the bank was able to establish a quantitative relationship between employee tenure and business outcomes such as revenue per customer and market share. Several other HR measures, such as expanded incentive compensation and targeted increases in managerial spans of control, were shown to have significant impact on business outcomes, ranging from reduced staff turnover and greater operating efficiency to lower payroll expenses.

It is well known that what employees say is not always what drives their behavior. This say-do disparity implies that human-resource decisions that rely solely on surveys, focus groups and exit interviews can be quite risky and costly. Companies invest millions of dollars in surveys and exit interviews in an effort to understand what employees value, what they like and don't like about the company, and what keeps them in the job. But few companies have made an effort to dig deeper for the actual records of stay and leave decisions: what the employees do and the context in which those decisions are made.

One exception to this, however, was one of the largest US banks in the northeast region. In the late 1990s, the bank experienced a high voluntary turnover which was costly and disruptive to the business operations. The bank conducted exit interviews and concluded that the high turnover was driven by dissatisfaction with pay. It then took a step further and examined the actual pattern of turnover over time to identify any antecedents of turnover events using a rigorous statistical modeling methodology. The analysis showed that, in fact, the factors that most influenced retention were whether an employee had been promoted during the previous year and whether the employee's supervisor had left. The bank's model showed that the voluntary departure of a supervisor led to a higher probability of the departure of his subordinates. The supervisor's departure acted as a catalyst for others to think about their own positions or security within the organization.

This new revelation led the bank to take on a more effective but less costly initiative to combat high turnover. It put more effort into communicating with managers and supervisors and started talking up the promotion potential and career opportunities within the bank.

FOCUS ON VALUE

The third salient lesson we learned from working with our clients is to focus on value. "People are our most important asset" is an often-heard statement in the modern corporate world. This statement implies that it is only appropriate to focus on the value-creating aspect of people and the activities and decisions that create value in measuring workforce and HR performance. Like any assets, human capital that can generate a stream of positive returns has a value. The value fluctuates, depending on the extent to which an organization is prepared to invest in people through such activities as position rotation and training. The personal choices employees make — to stay or leave, to learn or not to learn — also shape the value-producing capability of an organization's human capital. Company policies and practices can influence those decisions but cannot control them.

However, the reality is that most organizations still manage their human capital as a cost to be minimized rather than as a value-producing asset. This is because they only know how to measure people as costs or in isolation from business outcomes. The practice of benchmarking only reinforces the tendency towards cost management, as external benchmarks on HR or workforce performance are inherently focused on lowest-common-denominator efficiency and cost-based measures. Cost management has a natural limit: the floor is zero, but there is no ceiling on the potential value of human capital.

The experience of one major hospital chain in the US demonstrates how a value-focused perspective can improve decision-making on staffing.

In order to reduce business costs to meet the fierce competition in the late 1990s, the company had adopted the tactic of replacing full-time employees with part-time employees to save pay and benefits costs. This cost-focused tactic, according to the CFO, saved the company $5 million a year. Benchmarking the staffing mix with its rivals played a significant role in determining the mix of full-timers and part-timers for the company. In one hospital, 80% of its staff were part-timers. These employees were often less stable (that is, they had a higher tendency to quit) and were less interested in learning specific practices. As the number of part-timers increased, the full-timers had fewer career incentives.

However, when the staffing mix was analyzed in the context of its link to labor productivity at the facility level, the company was able to identify and quantify empirically the positive impact on labor productivity of a reduction in the system-wide use of part-timers. Immediately, the company had made substantial shifts back toward a more effective staffing mix. The resulting gain in labor productivity yielded $30 million or 3% of additional revenue on an annual basis.

Although this book has focused on the basics of HR measurement, we have also taken the opportunity to introduce a new HR measurement approach designed to help HR focus on the big picture in HR measurement. Based largely on our professional observation of companies that have moved along this learning curve, it provides lessons to keep in mind as you attempt to use the measures discussed in this book strategically. Importantly, the approach enables you to capture untapped value from your workforce, gains that can be translated into better business outcomes in either lower costs or higher returns for shareholders. Investing in people is no longer about hunches; it's about cause and effect. And it's about a competitive advantage that others can't copy.

CONCLUSION

In closing, we hope that this book has helped provide you with both the measures and the motivation to advance the HR metrics agendas in your own organization.

We have dealt with broad themes covering productivity, learning, staffing measures, reward and talent management measures. No one measure can be used effectively when used in isolation. The most profound benefits can only be gained from looking at your organization's contextual needs, and finding the measures that are relevant to your business context, market dynamics and organizational culture.

[1]   *Human Capital Management: The CFO's Perspective* (Boston: CFO Publishing Corporation, 2003), p. 11.

Appendix 1

MONITORING YOUR WORKFORCE USING HR "DASHBOARDS"

As organizations strive to keep ahead in a cutthroat global business environment, they are constantly being forced to re-engineer their business model to prevent being swept into oblivion by the shifting business landscape. Organizations which have in the past looked purely at investments in new machinery or technology to improve their business prowess are now taking a closer look at how they can invest in their human capital to harness the immense potential offered by the people within their ranks.

Business leaders and investors are also becoming increasingly focused on measuring costs and the subsequent return for every dollar invested in the organization. This has put pressure on HR professionals to provide quantifiable links to measure monies spent on human-resource programs and the returns on investments they produce. Unlike investments in physical assets such as land and building, the returns on investments in human capital have been hard to quantify, making it difficult for HR to justify the expenditure.

Expenditure on human resources is the single largest investment organizations make, yet it is also the one they know the least about. Given that measurement of the returns on human-resources programs has been something of an inexact science, HR professionals and business leaders have been less enthusiastic than they should be about HR measurement.

However, changes in the science of human-capital metrics are beginning to alter management perceptions of spending in this area. Earlier, we outlined some basic measures that can be used as a starting point to assess different aspects of workforce management. In the following section we introduce the idea of "dashboards" that will provide some guidance to companies that wish to keep track of the HR performance. Just as the dashboard of a car contains instruments that indicate how well or otherwise the vehicle is performing, so too these HR indicators will enable HR practitioners to monitor HR performance within an organization. It is worth repeating here that any organization attempting to use these measures should be very clear about both what it wants to measure and what outcomes it expects to produce. Once these have been clearly and precisely articulated, it can set about defining what these measures should be and how they are to be applied to the unique context of the organization.

One of the questions most frequently asked by organizations seeking to sharpen their performance is invariably: How do we get the right workforce to continuously deliver the business performance that we seek?

In this section, we will explore some of the issues affecting workforce productivity with the aim of finding how to use some of the metrics outlined in this book in the wider workforce-management setting.

UNDERSTANDING HUMAN-CAPITAL PRODUCTIVITY

Based on our work across many organizations around the globe, we have developed a view of some of the common drivers of human-capital productivity. The task of managing human capital has stretched beyond the traditional domain of HR management.

In 1994, Mercer Human Resource Consulting developed its own model of human capital based on more than 300 studies of how performance is affected by changes implemented across an organization's workforce.[1] What are the human-capital factors that affect a particular workforce's productivity and output? Our model is based on six broad factors captured in the human-capital wheel illustrated in Figure A1.1

Figure A1.1   The six factors that affect human-capital productivity

Research has shown that factors that drive workforce performance can be streamlined into six broad areas, namely, rewards; decision-making processes; information and knowledge about the business or job; management structure; work processes; and people factors. There are other drivers of productivity, such as culture and leadership, but their impact is embedded and captured within the six factors presented.

Rewards

This is the most explored component and has to do with how an organization rewards its employees, using monetary or non-monetary means. While rewards may not be the only component affecting productivity, it is nevertheless an important one. Whether an employee is productive also depends on whether the work is rewarding and whether (s)he sees an opportunity for career progression within the organization.

Decision-making

Whether an organization thrives depends on how visionary its leaders are and on how it positions itself strategically. Crucial, too, are how efficient and effective the organization's decision-making processes are. Employees also have to be mobilized in a timely manner to work towards the common strategic objectives based on the decisions made.

Information and knowledge

In the knowledge economy, how well an organization shapes the culture of developing information and sharing knowledge is a potent driver of success and productivity.

This factor deals with the how communication flows within an organization and the degree to which information is being channeled to all levels of the workforce. Easy access to information and knowledge can greatly enhance an organization's productivity.

Even the best of plans can end in total failure without a proper communication structure. An organization that has a great communication culture in place can quickly mobilize information for dissemination and for action. Proper communication channels supported by practical information systems can enhance the flow and exchange of information, and the creation of intellectual capital that can reinforce business success.

People

The core of any organization is to be found in its people. What type of workforce does your organization have? What are your people's capabilities? Where are the skills gaps within your organization? Are got the training programs in place to develop the skills needed? Do you have enough diversity within the organization? The answers to such questions can provide powerful information to improve workforce performance.

Work processes

This factor determines how well an organization's machinery is oiled. The work process determines how work gets done and the nature of an organization's production and service-delivery system; how different units function and collaborate; and the role of technology in shaping how the work is done.

Managerial structure

This aspect of the human-capital wheel deals with how people are managed — what kind of managerial systems are in place; whether roles and responsibilities are set out clearly; and how jobs are designed. The managerial structure also determines the extent to which the way employees are managed contributes to or removes their capacity do their work productively. The managerial structure should enable the organization to manage the performance of its workforce effectively.

BUILDING "DASHBOARDS" — DECIDING ON THE INDICATORS

Is there a quick and manageable way for HR to keep track of whether the programs put in place to drive better workforce performance are delivering the performance the organization seeks? Conventional wisdom has it that the sheer volume of information generated within an organization can be overwhelming and that there is little to be gained from having too much. Depending on how sophisticated your organization is in using HR measurement tools, it makes sense to start with deciding whether it is possible for you to build a basic system from scratch, or whether perhaps you should seek solutions from outside consultants, or even borrow from the ideas already being used by others.

The number of metrics that can be tracked grows by the day. HR benchmarks on their own provide limited benefits to an organization seeking to excel. Obsessive use of HR benchmarks against competitors or peers ignores the fact that every company has a unique organizational context. For an organization to gain full advantage from the range of HR information obtained, there needs to be an understanding of how to relate this information to the organization's wider business context.

What then should the HR "dashboard" look like? A practical approach to deciding what goes into the dashboard should be rooted in the basic principle that less is best. The dashboard should be able to provide meaningful information to HR for creating the desired business outcomes. A dashboard seeks to keep check of a few indicators to highlight either the success or failure of certain human-capital programs. The measures should also be robust and able to withstand rigorous scrutiny in relation to financial requirements and statistical testing.[2]

The dashboard tells a story of where the organization is heading in relation to a specific human-capital management plan. This could be a training and development program, a diversity program or a talent-management development program.

WORKFORCE MANAGEMENT — A BASIC FRAMEWORK

Figure A1.2. shows how a typical workforce management plan might look. It sets out the steps an organization can use to draw a roadmap to workforce management.

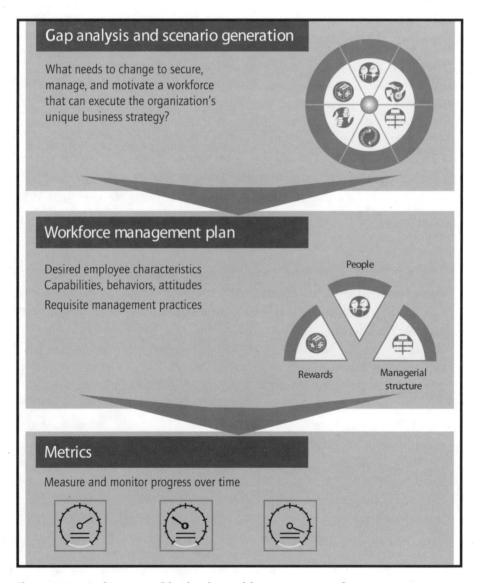

Figure A1.2   Seeking a sensible plan for workforce management[3]

Central to the workforce-planning process is making progress to move from the "existing" state within the organization to the "desired" state. This involves gathering information to help HR understand the organization's current state of affairs. The information requires qualitative (the organization's workforce practices, workforce attitudes and leadership perspective) and quantitative inputs (such as employee movements, rewards pattern and turnover). The desired outcome also has qualitative (such as leadership perspectives and selected external benchmarking) and quantitative aspects (covering statistical modeling of workforce characteristics and practices).[4]

UNDERSTANDING YOUR INTERNAL LABOR MARKET

Before progressing, it is essential to understand the demographics of your internal labor market. Figure A1.3 presents a profile of an organization's internal labor market, which can be loosely defined as the who, what and where of people movements within the organization.

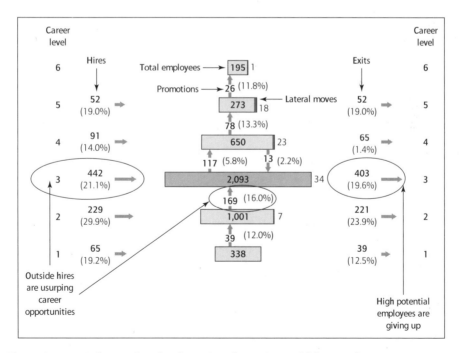

Figure A1.3   Understanding the dynamics of your internal labor market

Source: Mercer Human Resource Consulting

This chart presents powerful information to an organization about the possible causes and effects of its HR hiring and management policies. Coupled with factors affecting the external labor market, these analyses can provide useful indicators of how an organization's workforce is developing.

To understand an internal labor market better, more specific demographic indicators can be built, segmenting different levels of HR information specific to age, education, experience, gender and diversity, among others. An analysis of the internal labor market's variables provides a compelling picture of how the workforce behaves and why. These variables can include promotion, turnover, compensation, individual performance, lateral moves within an organization, pay levels and pay growth, among others.

Senior managers can use the rich data underlying an internal labor market to help them understand the attributes and behaviors that the organization values in practice.[5] Workforce information helps leaders and business managers find answers to questions such as:

- Do we have a workforce that can meet our future business requirements?

- What workforce practices do we need to maintain or change?

- How do we use talent management to help our business grow?

Answers to these questions will in turn provide a glimpse of whether the organization has the people needed to build a sustainable business.

METRICS TRACKING — WHY LESS IS BEST

The idea of creating workforce metrics may be an exciting concept but, far too often, there is a tendency for HR to go overboard with collecting as many metrics as possible. It is easy to get mired in the quicksand of HR measurement. The key is developing a practical HR metric system — one that can be easily implemented and managed.

One of the issues to consider in developing a practical set of metrics has to do with whether the measures are easy to construct and how easily available HR data is. These measures have to be easily understood by the staff as well as the business managers and leaders, and be free from selective manipulation. They also need to be consistent with the other measures used to gauge business performance in the organization.

Figure A1.4. contains a basic dashboard to monitor the effectiveness of an organization's return on investment (ROI) for training programs. The dashboard contains four main components: the employees' perception of the training (satisfaction index); the output from the training (achievement test scores); the performance rating of employees who have attended the training; and the impact of the training on the business (business outcomes index).

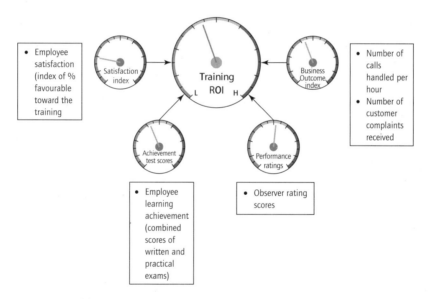

Figure A1.4   Dashboard to track ROI from training

It is important to build dashboards that always link back to the organization's wider business strategy. In the example above, one of the goals could be to grow the workforce fast enough to support the expansion of the business. Dashboards can help answer some basic questions about whether or not the organization is hiring fast enough to fill vacancies, whether it has sufficient human capital to meet business growth. The metrics that can help provide an indication of this include the time the organization takes to fill open positions (see Magic Number 19), the company's overall staff-turnover rate (see Magic Numbers 23 and 24) and the employee-engagement index (see Magic Number 21), which provide an idea of how satisfied employees are with the training programs provided. Similarly, for HR to meet goals of retaining high-performing employees, they would need to track the turnover rate by job performance (again, see Magic Number 23).

The reality in managing a dynamic workforce is that the variables within the organization change rapidly according to the changing dictates of the business. These realities are not always matched by the perceptions that exist within the workforce, as illustrated in Figure A1.5.

The organization's analysis of its internal labor market (ILM) shows that promotions within the organization are driven by training, performance and experience. However, results from an accompanying employee-engagement survey show that employees perceive promotions to be unrelated either to training and breadth of experience or to pay and performance. As a consequence, the organization has to take certain actions to fix the "perception".[6] These include keeping to the goals of its performance-management system, and ensuring that the workforce understands the system and how it relates to training and promotion within the company.

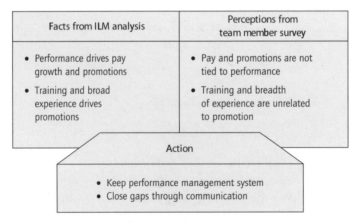

Figure A1.5   Linking perception to reality in the workforce

CASE STUDY: MEASURING THE EFFECTIVENESS OF TRAINING PROGRAMS

In the following example, ABC Bank is faced with the challenge of operating in a highly competitive business environment where a shortage of talent is a major headache for HR. In a high-growth market, the bank is faced with real and potential staff turnover as the job market is biased towards job seekers, who are not short of employers to choose from. To support its strategy of developing a high-growth business focused on customer satisfaction, the bank has invested in its training programs as a means to attract and develop a skilled talent pool. However, it doesn't really know how effective these programs have been, or how much return it is generating on this investment in training.

How, then, can the bank ensure that it develops a skilled talent pool fast enough in a rapid growth market while, at the same time, keep track of how much this expenditure is contributing to the business?

Basic building blocks

ABC Bank should adopt a two-step approach to solving its current predicament. Initially, it should take steps to determine the current state of its training programs, compiling information on the organization's training demands and the human resources needed to implement the bank's business strategies. This will reveal how the organization views the role training plays and the type of technology that will be required to deliver training programs. It should also be able to decide the business impact it hopes to achieve from introducing these training programs. Let's say, for example, that the bank wishes to reduce the level of risk it assumes. To achieve this, it needs to improve its internal credit-management processes by focusing on training employees in risk-assessment and credit-appraisal techniques (see Figure A1.6). The training programs can be built around improving employees' knowledge and handling of risk-management tools, or improving their investigative and financial impact-analysis skills.

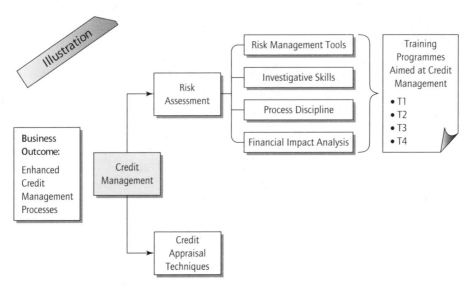

Figure A1.6. Focusing on components of training

Having set up the broad objectives for its training programs, the company should also draw up a list of the barriers that currently exist within the organization that could reduce the effectiveness of the training. By this stage, the bank should be able to develop a broad training strategy and map basic processes to achieve the program.

Next, the bank needs to build a dashboard for tracking the effectiveness of its training programs (see Figure A1.4). Such a dashboard should be able to reveal:

- whether employees view the training favorably

- what has been achieved by employees who have undergone the training

- the performance ratings of these employees

- what changes to the business have been effected as a result of the training.

Figure A1.7 presents the process flow for ABC Bank's training efforts. HR can decide, after a period of tracking and measuring the performance, whether the programs introduced for the company's Commercial Banking Unit at City 1, have actually contributed to improvements in the organization, say, to its credit-management processes.

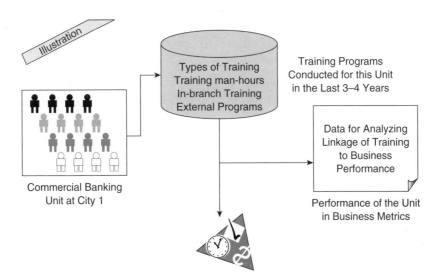

Figure A1.7   Linking training to business performance

It is equally important for the bank to build into the organization a process that changes how employees view their job or their promotion prospects because this is what contributes to or drives their performance. The company needs to ascertain whether the training has altered the way employees feel about their jobs or has increased their level of engagement with their work. It also needs to determine whether there is a link between those receiving training and those being promoted, and whether there is any correlation between training and staff turnover or between the performance rating and the training provided.

Based on the new insights developed from the data, ABC Bank will be able to build a series of predictive models to determine the problematic areas in its workforce and develop strategies to address these.

Getting a sense of returns from training programs

There are several approaches to calculating the returns on the investments (ROIs) ABC has made in its training programs. Some organizations use the "projected savings" approach, which takes into account the difference between the total administrative cost of the current training programs and that of the new training programs. Others rely on the "training spend" approach. This takes the total cost of training divided by the number of participants (see Magic Number 27). On another level, some organizations use the "predictive ROI" approach, which sets a target benefit/value to be derived from training programs. This is worked out by putting a monetary value on the net benefits of training divided by the total cost of the training program in percentage terms.

Concluding thoughts

In the final analysis, every organization that is seeking to design and build a sustainable business needs a high-performing workforce. Understanding what drives the behavior of your workforce is critical to managing your employees. (see Appendix 2)

Here, we have touched on some fundamentals that we see as important factors driving workforce productivity and performance. The human-capital model seeks to provide a framework for organizations to use in understanding some of the factors that are crucial to business success.

Human-capital measurement has progressed to a state where there is more science to it than previously held. An organization seeking to measure the return on human capital needs to be comfortable running a system that is practical and easily understood by all levels of employees and management.

By building a robust process, HR can provide some answers to stake-holders on what the clear and demonstrable links between HR spending and business outcomes. The overriding principle is that human-capital factors and business outcomes are closely connected. HR measurement seeks to explain how human capital is contributing to the business. It also seeks to address any gaps and weaknesses in the workforce that can interfere with high business performance.

In building such analytical tools, however, it is essential to remember that there is no single way to manage your human capital. What is best for one organization may not work for another, even within the same industry. What drives a business and what drives the human capital within it varies greatly from one organization to the next. Context is everything.

Linking human-capital factors to the business helps answer questions related to how talent is acquired within an organization, who stays, how leadership is developed, how performance is being managed, how rewards are being offered or made available to employees, and what the future shape of an organization's workforce will be. Understanding all these critical components will give HR the capacity to work on fundamental changes to human-capital management rather than simply applying patchwork solutions.

[1] "Workforce management that works", *A Mercer Point of View*, Mercer, September 2003.
[2] "Developing an HR LRP dashboard", Mercer Human Resource Consulting.
[3] This figure is based on work developed in a *Mercer Human Resource Consulting's Point of View* article called "Workforce management that works – New opportunities to leverage your human capital ". The *Point of View* contains ideas developed for a book called *Play to Your Strengths: Managing Your Internal Labor Markets for Lasting Competitive Advantage*, published by Mcgraw-Hill, 2003.
[4] Ibid.
[5] "Tapping the hidden value of people" by Tom Love and Haig Nalbantian, *Mercer Management Journal*, p. 16.
[6] This table is sourced from a Mercer Human Resource Consulting presentation called "Using employee surveys to drive business decisions — A look at the next generation of measurement", June 2003.

Appendix 2

WHAT'S WORKING AT YOUR WORKPLACE?

Are your employees engaged in their work? And are they committed to your organization's success? Do your employees have trust in the ability of your organization's leaders to steer the company through turbulent economic times? Do they understand how their work contributes to business success? Are your organization's HR practices and systems aligned with its strategic direction? Are your HR policies or programs delivering the desired results to help improve your organization's business performance?

These questions are part of an analytical process that can help your organization determine whether it is operating at peak effectiveness.

As the Magic Numbers in this book provide benchmarks to help you measure the effectiveness of your HR programs, this section focuses on research into what drives employee engagement in Asia. We hope that this will enable you to gain some new insights on how to use employee-engagement index/surveys outlined in Magic Number 21.

A well-established body of research now demonstrates that the way employees view their work environment influences not only the quality of that work but also absenteeism and staff turnover within the company. It also affects operating efficiency, customer satisfaction and retention, sales performance and returns for shareholders.

Employees who are actively engaged in their work, who are inspired by good leadership and guided by sound management, and equipped with the right tools and managed by the right systems and processes deliver superior performance and ensure business success.

The caveat here, again, is that each organization has a different operating environment, history, strategy and workforce characteristics. Developing an optimal human-capital strategy requires a precise and accurate understanding of what your employees think and feel. Properly designed employee surveys can provide this information and equip you with a critical tool to manage your employees.

What's Working in Asia

Many Asian organizations do not understand what drives their employees' commitment or what factors generate motivation and loyalty at work. There is increasing evidence to show that employees leave their jobs when they lack commitment.

Given that pay-related matters are often a source of discontent in Asia, organizations need to improve their communication on what drives pay policies and how pay is linked to performance.

This and other findings are based on surveys conducted by Mercer in China, India, Japan, Korea and Singapore. The survey also covered Australia and the US. The survey's 125 questions elicit views in areas such as training and development, work environment, leadership, performance management, work/life balance, communication, compensation, benefits, commitment and engagement, among others.

Asian organizations also seem to be struggling with performance measurement and the ability to deliver training and development programs to meet their employees' career-path needs.

Employees in Asia are motivated by different factors but a common thread is their wanting to be recognized and rewarded for their efforts. In places such as Japan and Korea, where massive restructurings have taken place, there is more evidence of employees' mistrust of management. While the Koreans struggle with the concept of trust,

Chinese employees tend to place great trust in their leaders and managers.

Although employees in India and China are generally happy with their work environment and infrastructure, they are less happy with their companies' lack of focus on their training or career-development needs.[2]

Given the developing nature of the labor market, it is not surprising that countries such as China and India had employees who were more committed to their employer, despite giving low ratings to their organization's pay and benefits programs.

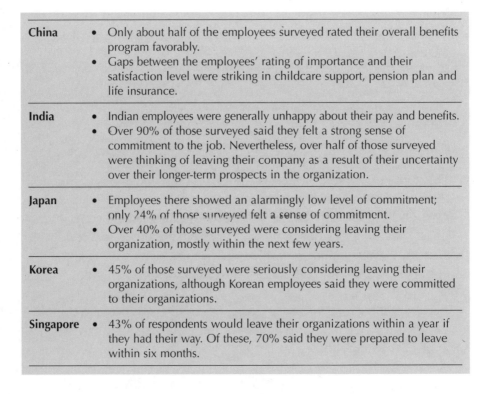

China	• Only about half of the employees surveyed rated their overall benefits program favorably. • Gaps between the employees' rating of importance and their satisfaction level were striking in childcare support, pension plan and life insurance.
India	• Indian employees were generally unhappy about their pay and benefits. • Over 90% of those surveyed said they felt a strong sense of commitment to the job. Nevertheless, over half of those surveyed were thinking of leaving their company as a result of their uncertainty over their longer-term prospects in the organization.
Japan	• Employees there showed an alarmingly low level of commitment; only 24% of those surveyed felt a sense of commitment. • Over 40% of those surveyed were considering leaving their organization, mostly within the next few years.
Korea	• 45% of those surveyed were seriously considering leaving their organizations, although Korean employees said they were committed to their organizations.
Singapore	• 43% of respondents would leave their organizations within a year if they had their way. Of these, 70% said they were prepared to leave within six months.

Although the conventional view is that trust is a commodity held in high esteem in Asia, employees place different levels of trust on the people they work for.

China	• There is a tendency to place trust and confidence in senior management.
	• Nearly 70% of the employees surveyed said they trusted their management to always communicate honestly, while three-quarters said their organization was well managed.
India	• Employees in India also had strong confidence in their senior management.
	• They believed their leaders were running the organization well and were in touch with the workforce.
	• Almost 80% of those surveyed believed their organizations would have a successful future.
Japan	• 20% of the employees said they felt that their managers showed concern for their well-being, while 22% said their managers understood their job-related problems.
	• Only 28% of Japanese employees said they thought their organizations were well managed.
Korea	• Trust in management was thin. Three out of 10 employees surveyed felt that their managers had concern for their well-being or understood the problems they faced in their jobs.
	• About 70% of the employees surveyed did not trust their management's communication. A majority of items in the survey relating to leadership in Korea showed low scores. Employees felt management's behavior was not consistent with the company's values.
	• Korean employees also believed that their department and organization were poorly managed. They felt senior management did not do a good job in managing the organization or in confronting the issues. Only 37% of employees thought their organizations would be successful in the future.
Singapore	• 40% of those surveyed felt their managers were honest in their communication with staff.

Given that places such as Japan and Korea have had a tradition where people stayed with a company for life, it is not surprising that job security is a major concern in these two countries. In Korea, only 37% of those surveyed said their organization would be successful and only 34% felt that it provided a clear vision for the future.

Only about 40% of the respondents in Singapore felt that they had a long-term future with their organizations. This is not surprising given that talent retention seems to be a common problem for many organizations.

Across Asia, there seems to be a need to build better links between reward expectations and how performance is being measured or communicated. Employees in all the countries surveyed had low ratings on how favorable their pay was.

China	• One in 10 felt that their performance was not rewarded for a job well done. • 90% said they were motivated by their company's reward/incentive plan.
India	• Indian employees were also motivated by pay. • Managers were given a low rating for their ability to properly differentiate performance and to ensure that the rewards matched the performance. • Employees in India also felt left out in training and development opportunities to match their career-development needs.
Japan	• Employees had a high level of dissatisfaction with the reward system. • Only 35% said their performance was recognized, while 21% said they were properly rewarded for their performance.
Korea	• 75% of employees felt that their pay level was not competitive compared to those of other organizations. • One in four felt that they were not properly compensated for their performance or contribution. Korean employees also valued respect above financial rewards.
Singapore	• 40% of those surveyed felt they were compensated for their performance. • About 35% said their pay was equitable or competitive with the marketplace. • An overwhelming 94% said reward factors influenced their commitment and motivation at work.

A better approach to using employee survey data

There is a great deal of information available about how employees view a whole series of factors related to work. An organization can evaluate its own results against the norm. But what's the best way to use norms? Traditionally, norms set a standard and become the criteria against which an organization can measure its own performance. The premise is that achieving or exceeding the norm represents the best approach for organizational improvement. A second approach is to combine normative data with historical data and a key-driver analysis to produce a more robust picture of how employees' perceptions affect your organization's performance.

Using this second approach, you can set priorities based on your understanding of the factors that influence organizational outcomes. Employee-engagement surveys can measure a whole host of indicators from how engaged your employees are to their perceptions on leadership or operational issues. The results of surveys about their perceptions can be linked to business data such as sales performance, customer-satisfaction ratings and employee turnover.

Once you have identified what items are of priority, compare them against the norm and historical data to obtain a measure of your performance. You can judge whether your organization's pay scores are consistent with the normalized score for your country, or compare norms of several countries to check for cultural bias.

Scores above the norm are considered areas where you organization is performing well against the key drivers. Scores below the norm represent areas where you are not performing so well and can improve upon.

Conclusion

Organizations spend an average of 36% of their revenues on their employees and yet this is the one component of expenditure which CEOs know least about.[2] Decision-makers tend to have a poor understanding of the human-capital issues driving employee engagement and motivation.

Today, high-performing organizations invest a significant amount of time and resources in developing an accurate understanding of their employees' views and engaging them in dialogue. Human-capital research has become an activity that is integral to the management of information that provides decision-makers with direction for business planning. Context is important and every organization is unique. Understanding what engages the employee can be a powerful means to drive an organization's success.

Business leaders and, more specifically, HR managers have a variety of tools and methodologies they can draw upon to help them understand what drives the behavior of their employees, and how to raise their employees' commitment to the organization.

[1] Mercer's What's Working™ Survey is a global study that helps organizations identify national trends and perceptions of employees at work. The results are based on data collected from a statistically valid sample from a broad cross-section of industries, weighted to represent a country's specific workforce. This chapter is based an article that first appeared in Mercer Human Resource Consulting's public website www. mercehr.com and excepts from the Singapore What's Working™ Survey.
[2] These and other findings can be found in Mercer Human Resource Consulting's What's Working™ studies published in 2004. The study is aimed at providing organizations with insight into their workers' attitudes and factors that drive their engagement.
[3] CFO Research/Mercer 2002 study.

Index

Other Titles in the
M A G 1 C
NUM8ERS Series...

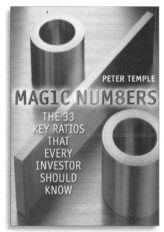

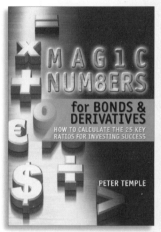